Start Now

Because no one will build
your security for you

Christelle Donhossou

Start Now

Because no one will build your security for you

Published by SheGrows Publishing

Geneva, Switzerland

ISBN (hardcover): 979-8-9963949-3-7

ISBN (paperback): 979-8-9963949-4-4

ISBN (ebook): 979-8-9963949-5-1

First edition — 2026

This book is offered for informational and educational purposes. It does not constitute personalized financial, legal, or tax advice. For any decision affecting your situation, consult a qualified and independent professional.

shegrows.ch

Contents

For my son, so that he understands that to love is also to protect.

For my daughter, whom I will teach how to build.

To the one who reminded me that certain truths deserve to be written,
even when they still tremble.

To my family and my friends,

for your love, your patience, and your presence in the most silent seasons
as well as the most luminous.

A woman can be surrounded,
loved, outwardly protected —
and still remain profoundly vulnerable.

Because true security
is not born only of what one possesses.
It is born of what one understands.

How to read this book

This book can be read in several ways.

If you have the time and the emotional availability to read it from beginning to end, that is how it was conceived. The chapters answer each other, build upon one another, and tell a story — mine — whose deeper meaning emerges fully only in the whole.

But not every woman will read this book in calm. Some will open it in the middle of a crisis. Others between two meetings, late at night, in a time of confusion, exhaustion, or rebuilding. If that is your case, here are a few entry points.

If you are currently going through a separation, the discovery of debts, some form of financial opacity in your relationship, or a sudden loss of your bearings, begin with the Letter to Women, at the end of the book. Read it slowly. Then come back to the chapter on financial violence if certain situations feel familiar, or to the chapter on the brutal awakening if you are already in the process of leaving.

If you are trying to understand why, despite your intelligence, your work, or your income, you have never managed to fully take back control of your finances, begin with the chapter on the invisible financial inheritance, then with the one on silent delegation. These chapters speak as much about psychological and cultural conditioning as about money.

If you are mainly looking for concrete actions you can apply quickly, go directly to Part VI, on reconstruction. The Actions proposed at the end of those chapters can be applied independently of the rest of the book.

This book is not meant to be read as a manual of suspicion. It does not say you must live in distrust, control those you love, or turn every relationship into a power struggle.

If you live in a relationship where transparency is real and decisions are genuinely shared, then these pages are not a call to fear. They are an invitation to remain present.

In a healthy union, financial awareness does not divide. It enriches. Understanding your numbers, asking questions, knowing how decisions are made does not diminish trust. On the contrary, it makes it more lucid, more free, and more solid.

Finally, this book is not a therapy. It is a companion of awareness. Keep it within reach. Return to it when you need it. And above all — do something. Because in financial matters, inaction often ends up costing more than the mistakes themselves.

Prologue
The day I almost said no

Seven years earlier, I had lost almost everything. What I did not lose is the voice that asks the questions. And it is that voice that saved me.

In 2025, I was invited to speak at an event on financial education.

My first reaction was to refuse.

Not from lack of interest, nor lack of time. From lack of legitimacy — that tenacious, almost physical feeling that this place was not for me. Speaking about money implied, in my mind, a flawless trajectory. A path without error. An unquestionable authority. And that was not how I saw myself.

The friend who had invited me insisted. She introduced me to the other speakers: a very senior Geneva wealth manager, two women working at international organizations, and me. The more she spoke, the more out of place I felt. Their place seemed self-evident. Mine escaped me.

Why me? And why at that precise moment — the one when I was finally becoming aware of the full extent of the mistakes I had made in my own financial life? Every reflection revived memories I would have preferred to leave behind me.

***

I remember the Friday evening before the event. Lying on my bed, still dressed, without the strength to take off my clothes, I was mentally listing the arguments for and against. My friend was slow to reply to my last message — a barely disguised attempt to cancel. Just before midnight, she wrote simply: Please, come. It will be amazing.

There are moments in life when one longs to hide, to disappear, to stop being visible. And it is precisely in those moments that something calls us to speak.

I had prepared almost nothing. I was tired, heavy inside. And then, the next morning, something had shifted in me. An unexpected clarity. A kind of momentum I still cannot fully explain. I said to myself: All right. I'll go.

* * *

As I arrived in the room, one question turned in my head: what could I possibly bring to this?

The first question was addressed directly to me.

Why is financial education important?

I began to speak. Simply, without trying to impress or to go into the details of my story. I reminded the room that wealth is not the result of luck, nor of inheritance, nor of exceptional income. That it is built above all in the silence of daily life — through repeated decisions, sometimes uncomfortable choices, an ability to anticipate and to act with intention.

I said that too many women keep their distance from financial subjects, as if money naturally belonged to another territory. That understanding money is not becoming obsessed with it — it is ceasing to be subject to it. It is being able to protect, to anticipate, to choose, to build. Because wealth is not born only from what one earns, but from what one understands, from what one decides, and from what one dares to do over time.

I also said that we often believe, wrongly, that one must already be rich to invest. That many women exclude themselves before they have even tried. Whereas building wealth begins precisely where one is, with what one has. What makes the difference is never the perfection of the starting point. It is the decision to set oneself in motion — and to stay in motion.

These words did not come from books or podcasts. They came from my own story. From a silent, heavy breaking I was still struggling to free myself from. And perhaps that is why they were heard differently.

* * *

At the end of the panel, several people came up to me. Some to thank me. Others to ask questions. Others still to confide, with a modesty mixed with hope, their wish to be guided. Men too told me that financial education was not only a matter for women. The quality of the exchanges exceeded anything I had imagined.

That day, something settled in me with a clarity I had not anticipated: my experience, however painful, had value. Perhaps even precisely because it had been painful.

What one has not lived, one can study, comment on, teach. But what one has been through, one can inhabit — pass on with a depth that theory alone does not give.

* * *

Those who were listening to me that day could not imagine what I had lived through a few years earlier. How could a woman working in finance — knowing the mechanisms, the rules, the risks — have been a victim of financial violence? How could she have entirely delegated the major decisions of the household to her husband, without ever really looking?

That is precisely the question this book tries to answer. Professional competence does not automatically protect. The diploma does not protect. The salary does not protect. What protects is something else — something I did not have and that I would now like to pass on.

The full answer took me time.

This story was not only his. It was also mine. Some decisions had been made without me — but I had let that distance settle in without seeing it, without naming it, without questioning it. In recognizing my own absence, I did not erase what had happened. But I recovered something essential: the possibility of acting differently.

That is where the idea for this book was born.

* * *

I did not write it to expose my wounds or to settle scores. I wrote it to pass on what one sometimes understands only after the fact — so that other women may recognize earlier what I saw only too late.

This book was written to awaken. To shed light on mechanisms that are often invisible. To remind women, with rigor but without injunction, that financial freedom always begins with understanding.

It is not about teaching women to do everything alone. It is about allowing them never again to be absent from their own security.

This story is mine. But if you are reading it, perhaps it is to better understand yours.

PART I

What I inherited

Chapter 1 — What we absorb without knowing

The invisible financial inheritance

Before the adult choices, there are the childhood models. They are not taught. They are absorbed — silently, in the living room, in the low conversations, in the gestures no one explains. And it is precisely because they are not taught that they then resist information so strongly.

I was not born with the idea of building wealth. Money has never been the engine of my choices. What has always driven me is something older, more visceral: the need to feel safe.

For a long time, I did not make the connection between these two realities. Safety, in my mind, belonged to the realm of emotion — family, refuge, the arms of those we love. Wealth, on the other hand, belonged to another world: the world of serious adults, of figures and strategies. A world that seemed to function without me, and without my needing to understand it.

What I did not yet know is that my relationship with money was already being built. Silently. In the living room of our apartment, in the low conversations, in the gestures of my parents that I observed without deciphering. We absorb our first financial lessons well before receiving our first salary. And they are often the most stubborn.

***

My father was a diplomat. A discreet, rigorous man, with something unshakeable in his bearing. He did not speak much about himself, but he spoke about the future. Constantly. With an almost military precision.

I remember that notebook. An ordinary notebook, hardcover, that he placed each evening on the corner of his desk. He wrote down everything in it — every expense, every income, every financial decision, no matter how small. Nothing escaped it. Not a meal, not a trip, not a household purchase. That notebook was his way of holding the world under control.

He often spoke about building a house back home. Not as a vague dream, but as a concrete project, advancing, even at a distance. That house was more than a piece of real estate. It was a promise made to his family, a mark left for those who would come after.

At the time, as a teenager, I did not see it that way. I saw mainly the constraint. The sense that we sometimes deprived ourselves unnecessarily, that life could have been lighter. It is only much later that I understood: my father was not trying to restrict. He was trying to build.

* * *

My mother, she was everywhere and nowhere at the same time.

She raised the children, ran the household, organized our life in countries that were not her own, learned new languages, adapted to new neighbors, new schools, new codes. She maintained a balance no one ever asked her to explain — because everyone found it normal. She was there, and the household functioned. That was enough.

What I did not yet see is what it was costing her. And what it had taken from her.

My mother had no bank account of her own. She did not participate in the financial decisions of the household. My father gave her money for groceries and the needs of daily life — and that was how it was. It was not presented as an injustice. It was simply the way things were. In our environment, a man who managed his family's finances was a serious, protective, responsible man. No one seemed to find it strange.

Neither did I, at the time.

But there was a question that sometimes returned in my child's mind, without my really knowing what to do with it: if Mom and Dad ever separated, what would Mom have? Where would she go? That question did not come from a dramatic place. It came from a silent observation. From a worry I would not have known how to name, but that I felt.

* * *

Then, one day, something changed.

My mother announced that she wanted to work. Not because we lacked for anything. But because she wanted her own money.

My father did not understand. He asked her directly, almost with sincerity:

"Why do you want to work?"

And she answered, simply:

"To have my own money."

That sentence — I kept it somewhere inside me for years without knowing why it resonated so much. It was not an aggressive demand. It was not a declaration of war. It was something far more fundamental — the need to exist financially in her own right. The need not to have to ask for everything. Not to depend on a silent authorization for every decision that concerned her.

My mother found a way. Without work papers in a foreign country, she landed a position at the residence of an embassy. She started to earn. To save. To plan. She spoke of a plot of land in her home village, of a house to build, of a future that would finally belong a little to her.

I remember her joy at that time. A different joy. Not the joy of a woman one indulges — the joy of a woman building something of her own.

* * *

Then the money disappeared.

When the family went through a period of financial difficulty, my father used my mother's savings. I never had all the details. But I remember her tears. That silence which was not resignation, but something more painful still — the loss of something she had built for herself, and that she would not see again.

The justification came, as it always comes in such moments:

"I have worked for years for this family. Now it's your turn to contribute."

That sentence can seem logical. Until one looks at what it erases.

What my mother had not devoted to a paid career, she had given to us. To our education, to our stability, to my father's career. Without her, nothing of what had been built would have held together in the same way. And yet that contribution appeared nowhere — on no statement, no deed of property, no official document.

She had given everything. And everything could be taken from her.

* * *

I watched.

Without anyone teaching me, something settled in me. I was learning that some people build what remains, while others maintain what disappears. I was learning that a woman can be indispensable to an entire family and remain, despite this, profoundly financially vulnerable.

These lessons were never transmitted to me as such. They slipped into my life otherwise — through habits, silences, balances that no one questioned. Until they became an inner self-evidence.

That is what conditioning is. It does not look like a prohibition. It looks like common sense. It looks like something natural, familiar, ordinary enough that it is no longer seen.

Years later, when I began to look honestly at the decisions I had made in my own life, I had to accept an uncomfortable truth: I was not ignorant. I was conditioned. And the nuance is immense.

Ignorance is corrected with information. Conditioning, by contrast, resists information. It can coexist with diplomas, with intelligence, with a career in finance. One can analyze risks all day for one's clients and reproduce, in the evening at home, exactly the patterns one absorbed watching one's parents.
I did it. For years.

***

What my mother taught me without meaning to

My mother worked, saved, planned. And she lost everything — not because she was naïve, but because she did not have the tools to protect what she had built. These rules are the ones I would have wanted to give her.

Rule 1. Love does not replace financial presence. Trusting one's partner is essential. But trust should never mean absence, silence, or ignorance. Knowing the accounts, understanding the decisions, earning one's own income — this is not putting the relationship into question. It is staying present in one's own life.

Rule 2. Savings without protection can disappear overnight. Before setting money aside, you must know in whose name the account stands, who has access to it, and what happens if the relationship changes. Unprotected savings are not savings — they are a fragile promise.

Rule 3. Invisible work has real economic value. Raising children, running a household, supporting the other's career: all of this creates value. In Switzerland, a stay-at-home mother replaces on average between 90,000 and 120,000 francs of services per year. If that value is not recognized in your couple, it is being silently drawn from your future.

Exercise. Three questions about your financial history: in your family of origin, who earned the money? Who decided how it was used? Who actually owned what was being built? These three answers often say more about our relationship with money than our first salary does. That is where the work begins.

No one will build your security for you.

PART II

What I reproduced

Chapter 2 — Working is not enough

The trap of income without construction

The models we absorb as children do not disappear when we leave home. They accompany us, silently, into our first adult decisions. And it is often in those first decisions that they cause the most damage — precisely because we do not yet see them.

After my high school diploma, I needed to leave. Not to flee, but to breathe. I had grown up in a structured, protective, sometimes suffocating environment, and something in me was demanding space — space to fail without witness, to learn without a safety net, to begin to exist on my own.

Morocco was my first real confrontation with money. Not with the idea of money — that one I had absorbed since childhood. But with its physical, daily, constraining reality.

My scholarship was insufficient. I could not work legally. And for the first time in my life, I had to borrow. Until then, money had always existed around me as a structure managed by others — invisible, silent, reliable. There, it suddenly became personal. Urgent. And fragile.

I discovered something the economics books do not always explain clearly: the one who lends is never entirely neutral. Even when they help with sincerity. There is in the act of borrowing something that subtly modifies the relationship — a balance of power that installs itself almost without intention, a slight dependence that changes the way one stands.

It is not a question of ill intent. It is a question of structure.

* * *

Proverbs 22:7

"The borrower is slave to the lender."

Years later, when I read that verse for the first time, it did not teach me something new. It put words on something my body had already understood in Morocco. That sensation of discomfort, of no longer being entirely free, of having to take another person into account in each of my decisions — that was it.

I made myself a silent promise that day: never again build my life on financial dependence. What I did not yet know is that this promise would only protect me from visible debt. Not from invisible vulnerability.

***

After my studies in Morocco, I left for Paris to prepare a master's degree. And it is there, in the 18th arrondissement, that I received my first real salary.

I had just joined one of the most respected audit firms in the world — a Big Four — where I had landed a position following an internship completed during my studies. That morning, when I saw the figures appear on my bank statement, I felt something I had never felt before. An almost physical joy. A relief. The sense that everything that had been sown over the years — the studies, the sacrifices, the moves, the uncertainties — had finally produced something concrete.

It was the symbol of independence. The beginning of adult life. The proof that I existed by myself, financially.

And then I spent.

***

My relationship with money was deeply emotional. Money served to live, to love, to circulate. It served to take the train to Geneva on weekends to see my family and the man who would later become the father of my children. It served to support those close to me, to buy clothes, to meet the immediate needs of daily life. To finance my sister's studies. To be present for those who mattered.

But it never served to build.

My parents had tried to pass something on to me. They often repeated:

"You don't spend a salary in full. You have to build something. Buy a house. Prepare for the future."

But in my mind, their words belonged to another reality. Their reference point was Africa, the projects back home, the construction over there. I lived in Europe, and without even realizing it, I reduced their advice to a geographical context instead of understanding its universal principle. And yet I could have applied exactly the same logic in France, then in Switzerland. It was not geography that mattered. It was vision.

And that vision, I did not have.

***

When I arrived in Geneva to work at a new audit firm, I continued in exactly the same way. My money served expenses, the home, daily life. Savings, when they existed, were only meant for emergencies — a minimal safety cushion, never a strategy. The notion of investment, of placement, of acquiring assets or building wealth was not even part of my reasoning.

It was not negligence. It was a system of values — inherited, internalized, never questioned. In many African cultures, and beyond, money is intrinsically collective. It circulates. It serves the group. Keeping for oneself what one could give to others can even seem selfish. This model has a real beauty. It speaks of solidarity, of belonging, of reciprocity. But it also has a cost no one calculates: that of one's own security sacrificed in the name of others.

I worked, after all, in an audit firm. I was surrounded by banks, balance sheets, wealth strategies. Words like diversification, asset allocation, and risk-adjusted return were part of my daily vocabulary. And yet — never had I asked myself what my own money was building for me. The thought simply did not cross my mind.

* * *

What the figures say

According to a UBS study from 2023, 57% of Swiss women report leaving investment decisions to their partner. In France, one woman in two says she has never invested on her own initiative. And yet, studies show that when women do invest, they obtain on average higher returns than men — mainly because they take fewer uncalculated risks and stay invested longer. The problem is not capacity. It is the inner permission to allow oneself.

There is a distinction no one had ever explained to me, and which would have changed everything: the difference between earning and building.

Earning means producing income. It is necessary. It is the starting point. But it is insufficient. Building means deciding that each month, a part of what one earns will not be consumed — it will be put to work. Invested. Protected. Directed toward a future one has chosen.

These two skills do not come together. One can excel in one and completely ignore the other. That is precisely where many women find themselves caught — not because they don't work enough, but because no one ever taught them the second part.

Morgan Housel, in The Psychology of Money, writes that wealth is what you do not see — the cars you don't buy, the vacations you don't take, the spending you postpone in order to invest instead. Wealth is not income. It is what income allows you to build when you do not consume it entirely.

***

I do not regret having helped others.

I am even deeply proud to have financed my sister's studies, to have supported some members of my family when I could. I continue to believe that money is not only for oneself. It can become a tool to help others grow, to open doors, to create opportunities.

What I do regret, on the other hand, is not having helped with consciousness.

Not having understood that helping others should not mean forgetting myself. That I could support my family while paying myself first. That it was possible to be generous and to build at the same time. That solidarity and financial responsibility do not stand opposed — they complement each other.

There is even a rule that finance professionals know well, often used in the safety instructions of airplanes: in case of decompression, put on your own oxygen mask before helping others. Not from selfishness. Because you cannot help if you have fainted. The image is simple. The financial lesson is just as simple.

You do not build for others by ruining yourself. You help them more, and over the long term, when you have built something solid from which you can give — freely, durably, without impoverishing yourself.

My mother had taught me how to work. No one had taught me how to build.

And that distinction, I paid dearly for.

* * *

What my first salaries taught me too late

Working is necessary. Building is indispensable. These are two different gestures — and the second one is learned.

Rule 4. Income does not automatically create wealth. Earning money and building financial security are two distinct skills. One is learned in life. The other is rarely learned — and that is precisely why it makes the difference.

Rule 5. Emotional spending can empty an entire financial life. Helping one's family, supporting one's partner, giving pleasure: these are beautiful gestures. But if all the money goes to others without any portion being set aside for one's own future security, one ends up generous — and vulnerable.

Rule 6. Helping with awareness is not helping less. It is helping better. Paying yourself first is not an act of selfishness. It is a condition for being able to give over time. You help others more when you do not need them in order to survive yourself.

Rule 7. The first investment is identity, not finance. The day you decide that a part of your money builds for you, something changes inside. You stop seeing yourself only as someone who earns and spends. You start seeing yourself as someone who builds.

Action 1. This month, open a separate savings or investment account, only in your name. Put into it a deliberately simple amount: 50, 100, or 200 francs depending on your reality. The amount matters little. What matters is the rupture this gesture creates: for the first time, a part of your money will not be consumed or given. It will build for you.

Action 2. Before deciding how much you can give this month to your family or your loved ones, decide first how much you keep for yourself. Pose the question in that order — not the other way around. This change of sequence is one of the most transformative gestures you can make.

Chapter 3 — Participating is not owning

What love never calculates

Working had given me an income. Not wealth. What I did not yet know is that in a couple, that distinction would dig a gap between us much wider than the one I saw on my bank statement.

He was older. More established. He spoke of investment with a natural ease, the way others speak of the weather. By his side, I felt safe — that safety I had been seeking since childhood and had never quite found by myself.

Without my realizing it, a transfer took place. I confided in him much more than a relationship. I confided to him, silently, the responsibility for our financial security. It seemed logical. He earned more. He knew. And somewhere inside me, I still believed that those who know can take care of everything in our place.

We never sat down to talk about money. Not really. There was no shared strategy, no common vision. The roles installed themselves without anything being decided explicitly. He managed the taxes, the investments, the major decisions. And I managed everything else — childcare costs, the children's clothes, the groceries, the cleaning, the invisible organization that keeps a family standing day after day.

I did not yet see the fundamental difference between what each of us did with our money. We were both contributing to the family. That seemed fair.

* * *

The yogurt pots theory — Titiou Lecoq

In her essay Libérées (2017), the French journalist Titiou Lecoq describes this mechanism with a precision that disturbs: in many couples, one person finances daily life — the yogurt pots, the diapers, the school supplies, everything that is consumed and forgotten — while the other finances durable assets: real estate, savings, investments. What is consumed disappears. What is invested remains. And when the relationship ends, a brutal reality appears: one person still owns something. The other has simply allowed life to function.

He invested in what remained. I financed what disappeared.

The house. The car. The assets capable of being resold, appreciated, passed on — all of this was being built on his side. My money, by contrast, supported the present. The immediate daily life. The constant needs of a living family.

It was not malevolence. It was an organization that seemed natural. And that is precisely why it was dangerous — because it did not resemble anything alarming.

***

The acquisition of the house was the first major purchase in which I really participated. At the time, it represented something immense. An adult milestone. The materialization of a family life we were building.

I looked at that house with the eyes of love. Not with the eyes of the law.

In my mind, it was our house. The fact that only his name appeared on the deed of property seemed to me neither strange, nor unjust, nor even problematic. It seemed almost natural — because deep down, I was unconsciously reproducing what I had seen throughout my childhood.

At my parents' home, there was no logic of permanent separation between what belonged to one and what belonged to the other. My mother contributed in a multitude of ways: by her work, her presence, her energy, her management of the household, the education of the children, the silent sacrifices of daily life. I had never grown up with the idea that a woman must necessarily appear on a notarial deed for her contribution to have value.

But life does not work that way. And the law does not either.

* * *

Then one day, the father of my children asked me to participate in the monthly payments for the house.

I still remember the disturbance this caused in me. Not anger. Not indignation. Disturbance. Because a part of me understood the logic: we lived together, we were building a family. But another part of me felt a deep unease I could not yet clearly articulate.

I remember thinking about it for several days. Something bothered me, even though I did not yet master the financial or legal concepts that could have explained precisely what I felt. And then this thought became impossible to ignore:

This house legally belonged to him. Not to me.

That meant every monthly payment increased his wealth. His asset was being built progressively, repayment after repayment. But me — what was I building, exactly?

If I participated in the monthly payments without being an owner, that amounted to financing a property that would never belong to me legally.

And if one day the house were sold, nothing would legally require any sum be returned to me.

That reality created in me an inner fracture. Because emotionally, this house represented our family. But legally, it belonged to a single person.

That is often where the greatest financial confusions in couples begin: when love gives an impression of total fusion, while the law, on its side, continues to distinguish precisely between the two estates.

I finally said no. But with hindsight, I see that this refusal was still imperfect. It was not a refusal built on real knowledge of my rights. It was an instinctive refusal, deeply influenced by my history, by my models, by my intuition. And that intuition was right — for reasons I could not yet quite articulate.

What is remarkable, by the way, is that I had perceived the imbalance even before I had the words to describe it.

The body often understands what the mind has not yet learned.

***

What the figures say

In Switzerland, according to a Credit Suisse study published in 2022, women own on average 40% less wealth than men at the time of retirement. This gap is not explained solely by salary differences. It is also explained by years of second-pillar contributions interrupted to raise children, by investments made in the partner's name rather than in their own, and by financial decisions taken without them. In France, according to INSEE, after a separation, the standard of living for women drops on average by 20%, compared to 3% for men. These figures do not describe exceptional situations. They describe a structural mechanism — silent, ordinary, and avoidable.

Many women live this type of situation without ever really stopping to reflect on the deep implications of certain financial decisions taken within the couple. Out of trust. Out of love. Out of habit. Out of family reproduction. Out of fear of damaging the relationship with discussions considered material.

And yet, knowing one's rights does not destroy love. On the contrary, it allows the building of more conscious, more balanced, more just relationships.

In every family, every financial decision engages much more than the present. It silently shapes the balances, the dependencies, and the securities of tomorrow.

I learned this in a way I would never have chosen.

***

What the yogurt pots theory taught me too late

Contributing to the life of the household is necessary. But it is not enough. Maintaining daily life and building wealth are two different gestures — and both must exist, simultaneously, in your name.

Rule 8. Participating in daily life does not mean building wealth. Expenses linked to children, food, family organization are indispensable — but they do not create durable assets in your name. Maintaining the household and building your security are two different gestures. Both must exist at the same time.

Rule 9. Love does not replace legal structure. A couple can be deeply in love and distribute their finances in a way that leaves one of the two people entirely vulnerable in case of separation. It is not a lack of love — it is a lack of structure. The two are corrected differently.

Rule 10. A woman must always be building something that belongs to her. Not from distrust — from presence. In every couple, a woman should be able to answer these five questions: What is being built? In whose name? How? With what risks? And what would concretely remain for me if the situation changed tomorrow?

Rule 11. Financing a property that does not legally belong to you is not a contribution to the household. It is a gift without legal counterpart. Before participating in the monthly payments of a property, an investment, or a loan, check in whose name the asset is registered — and what you would be entitled to in case of change.

Action 1. Mapping the household. Take a sheet of paper and draw two columns. In the first: everything you finance that maintains daily life. In the second: everything that builds wealth — in your name or jointly. Then ask yourself, honestly: if my relationship ended tomorrow, what would still belong to me?

Action 2. The five questions about any significant asset. For each important property in the household — home, savings, investment, vehicle — be able to answer: In whose name is it registered? What happens in case of separation? In case of death? Have I signed something that commits me? What are my rights? If the answers are unclear, that is the signal that a conversation — or a legal consultation — is needed.

No one will build your security for you.

PART III

What the system amplifies

Chapter 4 — The facade

Geneva, appearances, and the silent price of looking the part

Before the collapse arrived, there was the facade. The years during which everything seemed to be working — during which everything had to seem to be working — while something was already tearing inside.

Geneva is a strange city.

Beautiful, obviously. Orderly. International. Bordered by a lake that reflects the mountains. Clean streets, respected institutions, a reputation for seriousness and discretion that crosses borders. It is a city where people succeed — or at least, a city where people give the impression of succeeding.

And that is precisely where something deeply vertiginous lies.

In Geneva, appearance is not merely a vanity. It is almost a social currency. The car parked in front of the house. The neighborhood. The children's school. The restaurant where one dines. The vacations one mentions. The brand of the watch. The bag placed on the chair. Each of these details speaks. Each sends a signal. And in the circles where we moved — expatriates, finance professionals, binational families — these signals were read with a formidable precision.

For years, we sent the right signals.

And during those same years, everything was collapsing inside.

* * *

The life everyone could see

There is something particularly exhausting about maintaining a facade. It is not only the energy it costs. It is the permanent dissonance between what one shows and what one lives. Between the face one presents to the world and what happens behind closed doors.

I knew this dissonance intimately.

The dinners where we spoke of projects while the accounts were in the red. The outings maintained to avoid raising questions. The light conversations about summer vacations when I knew, somewhere deep inside me, that something was no longer holding. The carefully chosen clothes. The smile. The composure. All this invisible work of preserving the image — work that many women know without ever naming it.

Because in certain milieus, admitting financial difficulty is almost as painful as the difficulty itself. Shame sets in. And shame, often, drives people to spend even more — to maintain the appearance of someone who lacks nothing.

It is a cruel paradox: the more one fears being seen as someone who lacks, the more one risks actually lacking.

* * *

The city and its mirrors

Geneva is not the only city like this. London, Paris, Dubai, New York — the major international metropolises all share this particular quality of amplifying inequalities while making them invisible. The rich and the precarious cross paths on the same streets, sometimes frequent the same cafes, sometimes wear the same brands. The line between the one who owns and the one who imitates is not always visible to the naked eye.

But in Geneva, there is something additional. The concentration of real wealth — sovereign funds, private banking, international organizations — creates a benchmark that crushes everything below it. People compare themselves endlessly. They position themselves. They try to understand where they stand within an implicit hierarchy that no one ever formulates clearly but that everyone feels.

And in that context, the pressure to look the part becomes a structural force. Not just an individual weakness. Not just vanity. A real social pressure that drives perfectly reasonable people toward profoundly irrational financial behaviors.

People go into debt for cars they cannot afford. Families live in apartments too expensive for their real income, because the address is part of the image. Women carry bags that represent a month's salary, not out of caprice, but because in certain circles, not carrying them is a form of silent exclusion.

I do not judge. I have navigated these waters myself. I understand the pull of these mechanisms. What I want to name is their cost — a cost no one ever calculates clearly, and that always reveals itself too late.

***

The paradox of visible wealth

Morgan Housel, in The Psychology of Money, writes this counterintuitive truth: "When you see someone driving a nice car, you rarely think about the person — you think about yourself and how you would feel if you owned that car." Visible wealth rarely impresses those one believes one is impressing. It mostly impresses oneself — it serves to convince oneself of an image. Yet true wealth is by definition invisible: it is the decisions not made, the spending avoided, the money silently put to work. Those who appear rich and those who actually are only overlap in part.

What the facade does on the inside

There is a price no one ever mentions in conversations about money: the psychological price of dissonance.

Living one thing and showing another — even without explicit lying, even simply through omission, through modesty, through protection of the image — is a form of permanent effort that the mind cannot sustain indefinitely. The human brain is not built to manage durably a contradiction so fundamental between inside and outside.

The consequences are real. And they have a name.

Chronic financial anxiety affects millions of people in developed countries — including people with comfortable incomes, because the problem is not always the amount, but the dissonance between what one earns, what one spends, and what one shows. In Switzerland, according to a ZHAW study published in 2022, nearly a third of households report feeling significant financial stress — even among those whose income exceeds the national median.

This chronic stress has documented effects on mental health: sleep disorders, irritability, difficulty concentrating, a diffuse sense of shame, progressive isolation. People avoid conversations about money. They avoid friends who seem better off. They build invisible walls around their financial reality to avoid having to explain it.

And behind those walls, the situation often worsens — because you cannot solve what you do not look at.

* * *

Shame — the emotion that blocks everything

We have to talk about shame. Because it is shame, more than any other factor, that keeps people in destructive financial situations long after the moment when they could have acted.

The shame of not succeeding when one "should" be succeeding. The shame of not having seen. The shame of not having known how to manage. The shame of having trusted someone unworthy of it. The shame of having let appearances take priority over reality.

This shame is particularly intense in milieus where success is visible — where failure, even temporary, seems a betrayal not only of oneself but of everything one represents in the eyes of others.

I lived it. That sense of being unable to tell the truth because the truth would have destroyed the image. Not only my image — the image of the couple, of the family, of what we were supposed to represent.

And yet, it is precisely this shame that kept me too long in a situation I should have left earlier. Because leaving also meant admitting. Admitting to my family, to my friends, to my colleagues, to myself — that something had profoundly broken down.

Shame is the enemy of reconstruction. It paralyzes at the exact moment when action is most necessary.

* * *

The distorting mirror

This phenomenon existed before social media. But social media has amplified it in a way our brains were not designed to absorb.

Instagram, LinkedIn, Facebook — these platforms are showcases of filtered lives. You see the vacations, not the debts that financed them. You see the promotions, not the sleepless nights that preceded them. You see the smiles, not the morning arguments. You see the decorated apartment, not the consumer credit that equipped it.

And in the face of this continuous flow of seemingly perfect lives, a question settles in insidiously: why doesn't my life look like that?

That question, formulated or not, drives people to spend. To consume. To acquire visible signs of success in order to fill the gap between what they see and what they live. It is exactly the mechanism the platforms were designed — consciously or not — to amplify.

A study from the University of Pennsylvania published in the Journal of Social and Clinical Psychology showed that limiting social media use to thirty minutes a day significantly reduced symptoms of anxiety, depression, and feelings of loneliness. Not because social media is intrinsically bad — but because permanent comparison is psychologically costly.

And this comparison has a direct financial cost: it fuels impulsive spending, emotional purchases, the quest for material validation. Behaviors that impoverish over the long term those who could be building over the short term.

***

Living in agreement with oneself

Stepping out of the facade is not simple. It is not a decision one makes one morning that changes everything overnight. It is a slow, uncomfortable, sometimes painful process — because it implies letting go of a protection one built with care.

But it is also one of the most liberating acts I have ever accomplished.

The day I stopped fighting to maintain an image I could no longer afford — financially, psychologically, emotionally — something settled in me. A strange lightness. Almost surprising in the context of what I was going through.

Because the energy devoted to appearing could finally go elsewhere. Toward reconstruction. Toward reality. Toward concrete decisions rather than signals sent to an imaginary audience.

There is a word in English to describe this coherence between inside and outside: integrity. Not integrity in the moral sense alone — but the state of being whole, of one piece, without fracture between what one is and what one shows.

You don't get out of a facade by repainting it. You get out by leaving it.

***

What this chapter teaches — rules and actions

The facade has a price. Financial, psychological, and deeply human. These rules are here to name that mechanism — and to help leave it behind.

Rule 12. Appearance is a financial trap as much as a social one. Every franc spent to maintain an image is a franc that does not build. The question is not to live without pleasure — it is to distinguish what truly nourishes you from what only nourishes the gaze of others.

Rule 13. Shame prevents action at the moment when action is most necessary. Naming one's real financial situation — first to oneself, then to a trusted person — is often the first act of reconstruction. What you cannot say, you cannot solve.

Rule 14. Chronic financial anxiety is a signal, not a weakness. If money keeps you awake at night, if you avoid opening your bank statements, if you spend to soothe anxiety rather than from real desire — these are signals that something must change. Not in your personality. In your relationship with money.

Rule 15. Social comparison impoverishes. Not only emotionally — financially. Decisions made to equal, surpass, or simply not appear below someone else are among the most expensive and the least satisfying. The only useful comparison is with yourself, yesterday and tomorrow.

Action 1. Take inventory of your image expenses. Over the past three months, identify the purchases whose main purpose was to maintain an appearance — unworn clothes, outings you didn't really want to attend, disproportionate gifts, subscriptions kept for what they signal rather than for what they offer. Without guilt. Just to see.

Action 2. Speak about your real financial situation to a trusted person. Not necessarily to ask for help. Just to say aloud what is. Shame thrives in silence. It diminishes each time you name it in front of someone who does not judge.

Action 3. Limit your social media exposure for two weeks. Observe what changes in your consumption urges, in your anxiety level, in your perception of your own life. This is not a definitive experiment. It is a measure of the real impact these platforms have on your financial decisions.

Action 4. Ask yourself this question once a month: am I living according to my real values, or according to the values I believe I have to display? The gap between the two is often where the money disappears without leaving a trace — and without leaving satisfaction.

Chapter 5 — Switzerland and women

What happened to me is not a personal accident. It is a system problem.

For a long time, I believed what was happening to me was personal. Then I looked at the figures. And the figures tell something else: they tell of a system that produces, structurally, exactly what I went through — not only in my home, but in the homes of millions of women.

For a long time, I thought what had happened to me was the result of my own mistakes. Poorly made decisions. Misplaced trust. A lack of vigilance I should have corrected much earlier.

And then I started looking at the figures.

And the figures tell another story. Not the story of an isolated woman who failed. But the story of a system that produces, structurally and repeatedly, exactly what I went through. Millions of times. In thousands of households. With different faces, different stories, but the same outcome.

This chapter is not here to absolve individuals of their responsibilities. It is here to name what the figures reveal: that the financial vulnerability of women is not an exception. It is a rule.

***

The retirement gap — the figure that sums it all up

In Switzerland, women receive on average an old-age pension 37% lower than men's. Thirty-seven percent. This gap is one of the largest in Western Europe for a country ranked among the wealthiest and most developed in the world.

This figure is not explained by a difference in competence or intelligence. It is explained by an accumulation of mechanisms that activate one after another, often without the women affected being fully aware. Mechanisms that begin before the first job and worsen at each turning point in life — motherhood, part-time work, unpaid leave, an interrupted career.

And in the end, a 65-year-old woman in Switzerland receives on average 19,400 francs per year in combined AVS (state pension) and second-pillar (occupational pension) income. Her male counterpart receives 30,900. The difference — over 11,000 francs per year — is not a gap in merit. It is the sum of decisions that seemed reasonable, taken year after year, in the name of the family.

***

The childcare trap — when staying home seems logical

Switzerland is one of the developed countries where childcare costs are among the highest in the world. A place in a Geneva daycare costs between 2,500 and 3,500 francs per month depending on household income, after subsidies. In Zurich, the rates are comparable. In less urban cantons, places are as scarce as money.

The calculation seems simple. If a woman earns 4,000 francs per month and daycare costs 3,000, why work? The net benefit is almost nil. May as well stay home. May as well take care of the children. It is more logical. It is even more economical.

This calculation is correct in the short term. It is disastrous in the long term.

Because each year spent without contributing to the second pillar is a year that will never come back. Because each year of interruption reduces not only the accumulated capital but also the future pension rate. Because the part-time work that often follows this interruption — to remain available for the children, to accompany them, to manage the unexpected — continues to erode an already weakened retirement provision.

And if one day the couple separates, this woman who had made the reasonable decision to stay home finds herself with years of missing contributions, a diminished second pillar, and an earning capacity reduced by years of absence from the labor market.

She had made the right decision for her family. She pays the price for it alone.

***

The real cost of part-time work on retirement provision

In Switzerland, a woman who goes from 100% to 60% of professional activity for ten years loses not only 40% of her salary over that period. She also loses a significant portion of her second-pillar contributions — because the coordinated salary (the portion of the salary subject to the LPP, the federal occupational pensions act) is calculated based on the full annual salary. Below a threshold of 22,050 francs of annual salary (2024), income is not even subject to the mandatory LPP. Millions of women working at very low part-time rates are therefore entirely excluded from the second pillar — without knowing it. The Federal Statistical Office estimates that 59% of women in Switzerland work part-time, compared to 18% of men.

The matrimonial regime — what no one explains before you sign

In Switzerland, the default legal matrimonial regime is participation in acquired assets (participation aux acquêts). This means that assets acquired during the marriage are divided in case of divorce — but assets owned before the marriage remain the exclusive property of the one who owned them.

On the surface, this regime seems fair. In practice, it produces significant structural inequalities.

Here is why. During the years of marriage, the man often continues to work full-time, accumulating assets in his name, building a professional estate. The woman, on her side, works part-time or stops temporarily, finances daily life, takes charge of what does not accumulate. Her income disappears into household expenses. Her years of reduced work do not feed an estate — they allow the family to function.

At the time of divorce, acquired assets are divided. But if one party has acquired almost nothing in the legal sense, because everything they earned went to maintaining daily life — they have almost nothing to divide.

The law is neutral. Reality is not.

* * *

The figures of divorce in Switzerland and their consequences

In Switzerland, 40% of marriages end in divorce, according to the Federal Statistical Office. In major cities like Geneva, this rate exceeds 50%. The average age of divorce is 44 for women. After a separation, women's standard of living drops on average by 20% in France, according to INSEE — and Swiss data show similar trends. Men's standard of living remains stable or rises slightly. Alimony and the division of the second pillar partially compensate — but rarely fully — for the years of invisible contribution not valued by the law.

The second pillar — the ticking time bomb

The Swiss second pillar is often described as one of the most solid occupational pension systems in the world. For men who work full-time throughout their career, this is true. For women, the picture is different.

A woman who stops working for two years to raise her children loses two years of contributions. This is not only two years of missing capital — it is also the effect of compound interest on those contributions, projected over twenty or thirty years. A two-year interruption at age 35 can represent a loss of 40,000 to 60,000 francs of retirement capital, depending on income.

A woman who goes to 60% of activity for ten years reduces her contributions by 40% over that period. If her salary falls below the LPP entry threshold, she stops contributing entirely.

And if her spouse withdraws his own second pillar — to buy real estate, for an entrepreneurial project — and the couple separates later, the division of that pillar at the time of divorce only takes into account what remains. What has been spent no longer exists.

This is exactly what I lived through. Without understanding the mechanisms at the moment they were happening.

* * *

Beyond Switzerland — a European reality

Switzerland is not an exception. It is a revealer.

Throughout Europe, women are struck by what economists call the gender pension gap. The average across the European Union is 29%. In Germany, it exceeds 40%. In the United Kingdom, it is 38%. In France, it is 40% — but the universality of the pay-as-you-go pension system partially compensates.

What varies from country to country is the scope of the compensating mechanisms. France offers contribution credits for children, explicitly recognizing the professional cost of motherhood. Germany has introduced the Mütterrente, a pension bonus for mothers. Sweden massively subsidizes childcare to keep women in employment.

Switzerland, for its part, has long counted on the family to absorb the cost of motherhood. This model, which could have a coherence in a world where marriage lasted until death, no longer has one in a world where one marriage in two ends in divorce.

The world has changed. The system has been slower to adapt.

* * *

The women-men retirement gap in Europe (Eurostat 2023 data)

Switzerland: 37% · Germany: 42% · Austria: 41% · France: 40% · Netherlands: 39% · Belgium: 33% · Sweden: 27% · Denmark: 24% · Estonia: 4%. The Nordic countries show the smallest gaps — not because women there earn as much as men, but because active public policies compensate for the professional cost of motherhood: universal and affordable childcare, shared parental leave, social contributions maintained during interruptions of activity. The retirement gap is a revealer of public policy as much as of wage inequality.

What needs to be done?

The question is legitimate. And it deserves an honest answer — not a utopian one.

On the systemic side, several paths exist and some countries have already taken them. Massively subsidize childcare so that the economic calculation stops tilting toward leaving the workforce. Introduce contribution credits or bonuses for years devoted to raising children, as France does. Make parental leave genuinely shared, so that the professional cost of parenthood is distributed between both members of the couple. Revisit the LPP entry threshold so that very low-part-time workers — the majority of whom are women — are no longer excluded from mandatory occupational pension coverage.

These reforms exist. They are debated. They advance slowly. And in the meantime, thousands of women go through exactly what I went through — without a safety net, without information, without having understood in time.

These actions do not replace public policy. No woman, acting alone, can compensate for the thirty-seven percent gap that decades of structure have dug. If things are to change at the scale of Switzerland, they will change because many of us will be demanding it — through our vote, through the organizations we support, through the conversations we will finally agree to have publicly.

But while waiting for the system to evolve — and it will evolve, faster if more of us push — here is what you can do this week, at your scale, to stop letting the structure decide for you.

Stay in employment, even at a reduced part-time rate, so as not to exit the second pillar. Negotiate your activity rate before giving birth, not after. Check your pension statement every year. Understand the consequences of an early withdrawal of the second pillar before signing. Build a third pillar in your own name. Know your matrimonial regime and its implications.

These are not gestures of distrust. They are gestures of presence.

And that is exactly what this book proposes: not to change the system in place of the system, but to stop letting the system decide in your place.

***

What this chapter teaches — rules and actions

The financial vulnerability of women is not an individual exception. It is a structural mechanism. Understanding this mechanism is the first step toward ceasing to be its result.

Rule 16. Stopping work to raise a child has a precise, calculable, and often underestimated financial cost. This cost does not show up in the present. It appears at 65, in the form of a reduced pension. Before any interruption of activity, calculate concretely what that represents for your retirement — not only for your monthly budget.

Rule 17. Part-time work erodes retirement provision invisibly. Below 22,050 francs of annual salary, the mandatory second pillar no longer exists. If you work at a very low rate, check whether you are still insured — and if you are not, explore the options for voluntary pension coverage.

Rule 18. The default matrimonial regime in Switzerland does not automatically protect invisible contribution. The years spent financing daily life, managing the family, allowing the other to build — none of this is automatically valued by the law. Consult a notary or a lawyer to understand what your matrimonial regime concretely implies.

Rule 19. One marriage in two ends in divorce. A woman's financial protection cannot rest solely on the duration of the marriage. It must exist independently of the relationship — in her name, under her control, visible on her statements.

Action 1. This week, request your individual account statement from your pension fund (second pillar). This document indicates your accumulated capital, your projected pension rate, and any missing years. If you have never read it, start there.

Action 2. Open a third-pillar account in your own name if you have not yet done so. In Switzerland, the tied third pillar (3a) allows you to deduct up to 7,258 francs from your taxable income per year (2024). It is one of the rare tax advantages accessible to every salaried person. VIAC and Finpension offer low-fee solutions invested in ETFs.

Action 3. Before reducing your activity rate or stopping work, have your pension fund simulate the impact on your retirement. Most Swiss pension funds offer this service for free. A ten-minute simulation can change a decision that commits decades.

Action 4. Find out about your matrimonial regime. If you are married in Switzerland without a specific contract, you are under the regime of participation in acquired assets. Understanding what this concretely means — what will be divided, what will not be, how the second pillar is treated at divorce — is basic knowledge every married woman should have. An hour-long appointment with a notary is enough for the essentials.

No one will build your security for you.

PART IV

What I let settle in

Chapter 6 — The silent delegation

How one ceases, without seeing it, to participate in one's own life

The figures explain a system. They do not explain how one lives inside it. To understand how a woman who knew the rules could stop applying them at home, you have to go back to a specific evening. To a house. To a signature that seemed unimportant.

The problem was not only financial. Well before the losses, well before the risky decisions, something had settled in me — an almost instinctive belief, so deeply anchored that I no longer even saw it: the one who holds the money naturally knows best how to manage it.

This idea did not come from him. It existed before him. It had built itself discreetly, over the course of childhood, through the balances I observed in my family, the models I had ended up considering natural simply because they had always existed that way. Without realizing it, I had associated financial security with a figure outside of myself.

That shift, no one had taught me. It had simply settled in.

***

One of the things that hurt me most in my couple was not only money. It was the way decisions were made.

I had grown up in a family model where the man naturally carried certain responsibilities and where many important decisions seemed to fall to him almost automatically. My mother supported, accompanied, kept the household balance running with an immense but often silent strength.

Except I was not my mother. I lived in another era, in another country, in another context. And above all, I had a strong character, a capacity for reflection, a vision. Deep down, something resisted.

What I often reproached the father of my children for was not only the decisions themselves. It was the fact that they were already made before the discussion really existed. The reflections were carried out alone. The trade-offs were made alone. And then came simply the moment of announcing to me what had been decided.

For the daily subjects, this could pass. But for everything that had a major impact on our future — real estate, investments, strategic choices for the family — I was not really integrated into the process.

Now, participating in a decision is not simply being informed after the fact. Participating means being able to reflect together. To ask questions. To expose the risks. To weigh the advantages and disadvantages. To look at the possible consequences. To confront the different views. And only then to choose the path that seems most just for the family.

But this we almost never did.

* * *

I still remember the day I signed the sale deed of our family home.

I had just come back from work. I was exhausted. I still had my work suit on. In my head, I was already thinking about the evening meal, the children, everything that still needed to be managed before night. Like many women, I lived in that permanent mental load where every minute of the evening already belongs to family responsibilities.

When I came in, he had prepared the documents.

"I told you you had to sign some papers. It's important."

I had not even changed yet. My bag was still by the entrance. I was standing between two obligations, in that state of fatigue where one functions almost automatically.

"In Switzerland, you need to sign the sale deed."

And inside, I simply told myself: it's his house, he bought it, so I have to sign.

Even today, this memory disturbs me by the emotional neutrality I was in.

I did not ask questions. I did not ask for time to think. I did not seek advice. I did not even really read the documents.

Not because I was incapable of understanding. But because the functioning of the couple had progressively accustomed me to this. Major decisions often arrived in urgency. In a rush. Between two obligations. Without real space for discussion.

"You need to sign this."

"It's urgent."

"We need to do this."

And I followed. Because I trusted.

And that is probably where the deepest mistake lay. Not in love. Not in the will to build together. But in this dangerous idea that trust exempts one from understanding.

***

The Swiss second pillar — what many women ignore

In Switzerland, the second pillar — occupational pension provision — often represents the largest part of a couple's wealth. It accumulates during the years of activity and constitutes a major reserve for retirement. In case of divorce, the second pillar acquired during the marriage is divided between the two spouses — unless a different agreement is approved by a judge. In case of early withdrawal for the purchase of a home or for an investment, this money must be repaid if conditions change. Signing to authorize the withdrawal of a spouse's second pillar engages rights that many women ignore. Understanding these rules before signing is non-negotiable.

I lived through this too when he wanted to withdraw his second pillar to invest in his self-employed activity.

There again, I was coming back from work. There again, I had to sign quickly.

At that time, I knew almost nothing about the Swiss pension system. I did not really know what the second pillar represented. I did not know what protections or rights I had within the framework of marriage. So when he explained to me that he needed this money for his activity, I immediately thought: it's for the family.

In a couple, one does not spontaneously make legal or estate calculations. One thinks in terms of trust, support, shared project.

When he decided to sell our family home, then later the vacation home, the argument was always the same: to invest in his self-employed activity. And honestly, I sincerely wanted him to succeed. I believed in him. I wanted to support him. If sacrifices were needed to allow his project to grow, I was ready.

That is also what loving someone means: wanting their success profoundly.

But loving should never mean erasing oneself entirely from decisions. Because in reality, I had a say. And if I had had more information, more awareness of my rights and the legal implications of certain decisions, I would certainly have acted differently.

***

The psychology of delegation — what research says

The American researcher Kathleen Vohs, a specialist in the psychology of money, has shown that individuals who entirely delegate their financial decisions to others progressively develop what she calls "financial anesthesia" — a form of disconnection from their own economic reality. The more distance settles in, the less legitimate one feels to intervene. And the less one intervenes, the more the distance grows. It is a circle that closes silently, often over years, before a crisis suddenly makes it visible.

With hindsight, I see today a real pattern. A way of functioning that progressively installed itself in our relationship. I do not necessarily think there was malicious intent behind each situation. But there was clearly an imbalance in how decisions were brought up, explained, and executed.

The problem is that when things break, the gaze changes brutally. It is often after a separation that the real questions appear.

"Why did I accept this without asking questions?"

"Why did I never inform myself?"

"Why did I believe that understanding was unnecessary since I loved and trusted?"

Then come the discussions with lawyers, notaries, professionals. And that is where one sometimes discovers that certain decisions could have been made differently. That certain rights existed. That certain protections were possible. And this realization can be extremely painful — because it forces one to look in the face at everything one did not want to see. Or everything one had never learned to see.

What still troubles me today is that my intuition had been speaking to me for a long time. I sensed the imbalances. I perceived the inconsistencies. But I did not give that inner voice enough room. Because in a couple, listening to your financial intuition can resemble distrust. Because asking questions can seem to call the other's good faith into question. Because demanding understanding can pass for control.

These fears are real. And they are precisely what prevents many women from fully participating in their own financial security.

Understanding does not destroy love. Understanding protects the relationship as much as it protects oneself.

* * *

What the silent delegation taught me

Trusting is a strength. Being absent from one's own financial security is a vulnerability. The two can coexist for years — until the day when one no longer has a choice but to look.

Rule 20. Trusting never exempts one from understanding. Loving someone or recognizing their competence should never lead to abandoning the understanding of decisions that engage one's own security. Healthy trust coexists with visibility, with questions, and with a minimum understanding of the stakes.

Rule 21. Urgent decisions deserve even more attention than other decisions. Fatigue, mental load, urgency presented as self-evident — these are the conditions in which the signatures with the heaviest consequences are often obtained. Taking twenty-four hours before signing an important document is never a bad decision.

Rule 22. What one stops looking at ends up escaping. Accounts, credits, investments, fiscal commitments can progressively become opaque when a single person manages them. And the more the distance settles in, the more difficult — and painful — it becomes to return to it.

Rule 23. Listening to your financial intuition is not distrust. It is responsibility. If something bothers you about a decision — a document you are being pressed to sign, information that is slow to come, an explanation that remains vague — that sensation deserves to be heard, not stifled.

Action 1. The visibility file. This week, open a notebook or a digital folder titled My Financial Reality. Gradually gather: the accounts and their balances, credits and debts, insurance policies, investments, documents linked to retirement and to the second pillar, assets held in your name or jointly, the household's financial commitments. Then ask yourself one question, honestly: if tomorrow I had to explain our financial situation to someone outside, could I do it alone? If the answer is no — that is a signal. And it is precisely there that taking back your financial presence begins.

Action 2. Before signing anything important, ask these three questions: How much time do I have to read and understand this document? What are the consequences if I refuse or postpone my signature? Who can I consult before signing? A notary, a lawyer, a trusted friend, an independent financial advisor — a second pair of eyes on an important document can change the course of a life.

Chapter 7 — The silent disappearance

Geneva · first child · the first cracks

There was a moment, well before money became the problem, when I stopped being present in my own life. No one saw it — I myself was the last to. But that is where, I believe today, everything began.

I had given birth in one of the best clinics in Geneva. The setting was reassuring, the medical team competent. And yet.

The birth was very difficult. I came close to septicemia. I was feverish. My son spent several days on antibiotics. My body was exhausted in a way I had never known — but it is what collapsed inwardly that was the most lasting.

When I came home, I discovered a fatigue of another order. Not the fatigue of a sleepless night. Not that of a week of intense work. A fatigue that seemed to touch consciousness itself. I would wake up in the morning in an inner fog. As if I were physically present but absent from the inside.

I had no desire for anything.

This absence of momentum extended even to the most essential gestures. I had no desire to take care of myself. I had no desire to eat. Sometimes, I did not have the mental strength to think of feeding my baby on time. I did things mechanically. Without joy. Without energy. Without real presence.

* * *

I put no words on what I was living. I simply thought I was weak. Or incapable of managing this new life. And I stayed silent, nourished by that strange belief that the people who love us should guess our needs without our having to express them.

I thought my suffering was visible. I thought my exhaustion spoke for me.

It was not speaking.

I was alone. My mother was in Benin — my sister had given birth a month earlier and could not leave the country. My mother-in-law, who was supposed to stay several weeks, ended up staying only two days. And the father of my son, despite his paternity leave, was very little present. He used that time for other obligations. I found myself alone at home with a newborn, while I myself was sinking.

The birth of a child transforms everything. It makes a couple into a family. This shift should have brought us closer, forced us to organize differently, to think as two about what each of us had been carrying alone. But what this period revealed, on the contrary, is that we continued to function as two parallel individuals — each in our own world, each in our own responsibilities — while something entirely new had just been born between us.

The absence of concertation that I would experience in the years that followed had perhaps begun there. In that silence. In those first weeks when no one had named what was happening. Neither him. Nor me.

***

I remember the day my father came to visit.

He found my son lying on the sofa, without a blanket, without the small instinctive attentions a mother normally gives a newborn. And I was there — exhausted, disheveled, absent.

I believe it was at that moment that he understood something was wrong. What he was seeing went well beyond the normal fatigue of a young mother.

He took charge. He organized my mother's arrival from Africa. And it is there that I slowly began to come back to myself. To eat properly again. To regain strength. To find a little inner presence again.

But the trauma stayed a long time.

For nearly an entire year, I was incapable of looking at the photos of my delivery or of the first weeks after the birth. Each image plunged me back immediately into the pain of that period. When I looked at my face in those photos, I did not see a happy young mother. I saw a lost woman. Extinguished. Empty.

***

Today, I know I was going through postpartum depression. At the time, that word did not exist in my head. It did not exist either in the conversations of my surroundings. No one had taught me to recognize it. No one had taught me to ask for help.

I had been taught to hold.

Postpartum is a reality of which we still speak too little honestly. We show the babies, the decorated rooms, the first smiles. But we speak less of that sensation of inner disappearance that some women go through after giving birth. That strange impression of having given life while feeling, for a time, that one has lost contact with one's own.

***

Postpartum in Switzerland — figures that remain invisible

According to the Federal Office of Public Health, approximately 10 to 15% of women in Switzerland develop postpartum depression after giving birth. The vast majority receive neither diagnosis nor treatment — not because care does not exist, but because the symptoms are often normalized as ordinary fatigue, or because women themselves do not dare to name them. The postnatal consultation is reimbursed by basic health insurance up to 56 days after giving birth. The family doctor, the midwife, or the cantonal perinatal psychiatry service are the first available resources.

A woman who has just given birth does not only need practical advice. She needs to be carried, surrounded, emotionally nourished — and protected the time it takes to slowly find the light within her again.

This is not a luxury.

And no one had told me that asking for it was allowed.

***

Today, I believe that it is in those weeks that the voice that asked the questions fell silent for the first time.

Not quite extinguished. Asleep.

Once a voice has fallen silent, one learns to live without it. One learns to let someone else ask the questions. To let someone else decide. And without my knowing, I carried that silence with me through the years that followed — even into the financial conversations where it would have been vital to find it again.

The financial violence that struck me later did not begin on a day of falling stock markets. It began on a winter evening, in a Geneva bedroom, with a newborn in my arms and a young woman who no longer had the strength to ask for help.

This silence is one of the most invisible costs of untreated postpartum depression. No one calculates it. No one sees it. And yet, it can cost an entire financial life.

* * *

What this chapter teaches

Untreated postpartum is often invisible — to the woman herself and to those around her. These rules and actions are here to name what too often remains nameless.

Rule 24. Postpartum depression can last months and go unnoticed. Extreme fatigue, absence of momentum, emotional fog — these symptoms are often normalized. They should not be. If you recognize these signs in yourself or in a woman close to you, seek help without waiting.

Rule 25. Asking for help is not failing. It is acting. The belief that the people who love us should guess our needs without our expressing them is one of the most costly there is — emotionally, and sometimes financially.

Rule 26. A couple becomes a family at the birth of a child. This shift requires a conscious reorganization — not only logistical, but decisional. Who makes which decisions? Who is informed of what? Who signs what? These questions deserve to be asked aloud, not left to the drift of the implicit.

Action 1. If you are pregnant or have just given birth, speak to your doctor or midwife about postpartum depression before it arrives. Ask them how to recognize it and whom to turn to. The postnatal consultation is reimbursed by basic health insurance up to 56 days after giving birth.

Action 2. Before or shortly after a birth, take the time together to ask the financial and organizational questions that no one ever asks: Who manages the accounts during maternity leave? What important decisions are expected in the coming months? Who signs what? This conversation takes an hour. It can prevent years of imbalance settling in silence.

No one will build your security for you.

PART V

What I went through

Chapter 8 — Financial violence

What we do not see because we do not want to see

For a long time, I thought financial violence was something that happened to other people. To more naïve women. To less educated women. To women I could look at from a distance, with compassion, thinking: this could never happen to me.

Names like Kerviel or Madoff seemed to me to belong to another category of reality. The category of the great financial scandals discussed in newspapers and documentaries — men whose excesses end in highly publicized trials, in films, in astronomical figures the mind struggles to grasp. I did not yet know that silent versions of these dramas also exist. Collapses that destroy not institutions, but families. Decisions made behind the closed doors of homes. Invisible losses that slowly swallow the entire security of a couple while the rest of the world keeps believing that everything is fine.

And without understanding it yet, I was already coming closer to it.

* * *

What financial violence really is

I had imagined financial violence as something obvious to recognize. Women deprived of money, prevented from working, controlled in each of their expenses, living under a visible domination one could immediately identify as abusive. I have often wondered whether my mother would have stayed with my father if she had had her financial independence. The answer is clearly no. And I have always believed that the sacrifices she consented to were devastating — not because she did not love her family, but because staying without the choice to leave is not love. It is dependence.

A woman's freedom begins, essentially, with her financial freedom. A woman who works, who contributes, who owns something in her own name has a choice. She can stay because she has decided to. She can leave if the relationship threatens her balance. It was this fundamental freedom that I had decided to preserve, no matter what. And yet, despite this conviction, despite the job I kept throughout my life as a couple, despite my salary, despite my career in finance — I was about to experience one of the most destructive forms of silent financial violence. Because financial violence does not always begin with a prohibition. It often begins with opacity. With a fog that settles in so slowly that one ends up taking it for natural fog.

***

The first signs

I do not remember the exact moment when I stopped truly knowing what was happening in our shared finances. It did not happen in a single decision. It was more diffuse than that. A signature made quickly. A vague answer accepted because the children were asking for something at the same moment. A discussion postponed to the next day. Then to the next month. Then to later. Gradually, a financial fog settled in. And that fog had something deeply deceptive about it: it coexisted with a life that, from the outside, still seemed perfectly normal. The father of my children had left his job to go out on his own, relying on an asset he had discovered during his studies at prestigious American universities: Bitcoin. It was 2016. He was convinced of it with an almost religious certainty: this asset would one day reach 200,000 francs. At the time, it was fluctuating between 1,000 and 3,000 dollars.

His office had turned into a market laboratory. He followed the charts for hours, read, analyzed, exchanged. Our house had become a discussion salon on cryptocurrencies. Friends, relatives, everyone came by. Switzerland itself was positioning: Zug was becoming the Crypto Valley, attracting specialized companies with tax advantages. The stars seemed aligned. I was both curious and skeptical. Gold has value because central banks guarantee it. But Bitcoin? On what did that value really rest? He spoke to me of a historic opportunity with this new decentralized finance. Of financial independence. Of the future. Like many finance professionals, he believed he understood the markets well enough to master the risk. But financial markets are not only mathematical systems. They are crossed by ego, fear, overconfidence — that dangerous illusion that drives some people to believe they control something that remains profoundly unpredictable.

* * *

How you lose everything while still thinking you are right — leverage

Leverage means borrowing in order to invest more than you actually own. If you place 10,000 francs with a leverage of 10, you are in reality controlling 100,000 francs on the market. When prices rise, the gains seem extraordinary. A 10% increase can be enough to double the capital. This is precisely what makes leverage psychologically dangerous: at the start, it works. The problem appears when markets fall. With heavy leverage, a relatively small drop can wipe out almost the entire capital. The broker then demands new funds to keep the positions open — this is the margin call. If the investor cannot pay, the positions are liquidated automatically, often at the worst moment, when the markets are already in panic. The real trap is psychological: someone who has won big through leverage often believes those gains come from their intelligence, not from the context. When the losses begin, many do not stop. They increase their positions to recover what has been lost. That is often where the real collapses begin.

COVID, or the end of the fog

In Geneva, everything tipped over at the end of February 2020, when the first case of COVID-19 was officially confirmed. In just a few weeks, schools closed, the streets emptied, the borders tensed, and a feeling of uncertainty settled abruptly into the daily lives of millions of people.

Deep down, though, I still believed this period would bring us closer. I imagined that working from home, slowing down together, taking care of the children side by side would force us to find each other again, differently. I thought that with enough organization, lucidity, and goodwill, we would manage to weather this storm together.

But in reality, we hardly crossed paths anymore. He, shut away on the third floor in his office. Me, settled on the first floor, my back to the window looking out onto the rue d'Hermance. We lived under the same roof, but each of us already seemed to inhabit a different world. And between us, there were the children, lost in their online classes, trying as best they could to occupy themselves alone while we finished our workdays behind our screens.

One day, as I was preparing for an important presentation to my management, the internet connection cut out abruptly. In our municipality, that kind of outage happened sometimes. But this time, something was different. Impossible to restart the router. No signal at all. Then a message from Swisscom appeared on my screen: the line had been suspended.

When I asked for an explanation, the answer was simple, almost trivial: a missed payment. And yet, Swisscom does not suspend a line for a single month's delay. I tried to convince myself it was an isolated incident. But a few weeks later, the same scene repeated itself.

That time, something in me understood before I was even ready to accept it: he was no longer paying the bills. And despite this, my mind still refused to imagine the worst. The amount owed was trivial. A few hundred francs at most. How could a serious situation begin with something so small? Strangely, the connection was restored that same day.

But a few days later, the postman rang. A demand for payment. 45,000 francs owed to the Geneva tax authority.

In twelve years in Switzerland, I had never seen anything like it. My head spun. I almost fell.

When I asked him about it, he answered with that calm assurance that had always reassured me: don't worry, everything is under control. And he went back into his office.

I stayed lost in thought for long minutes. I had already entered that silent phase that is denial. The signs were beginning to accumulate, the inconsistencies becoming more and more visible, but my mind still refused to measure their real scope. It was impossible for me to imagine that a chasm so deep had already opened beneath our feet, ready to swallow everything we had built.

This episode clearly marked the end of the apparent security in which I still believed I was living. For the first time, a visible crack ran through the scenery I was struggling to keep standing. But I did not know it yet: this was only the tip of the iceberg.

***

The first crash

During that same period, world markets entered a zone of rarely seen brutal turbulence. What had started as a health crisis tipped progressively into a global financial crisis. Day after day, the screens turned red, the indexes collapsed, and uncertainty now contaminated economies as much as minds. In a few weeks, what many thought stable, solid, or predictable revealed its fragility in the face of an event no one truly controlled.

I did not see him all day. I learned later that on that day, he had lost thousands of francs.

That was the beginning of the collapse.

I saw him more and more rarely. And when we met for dinner, he was either calm or strangely cheerful — playing chess with the children, helping my son with his homework. It was impossible to suspect what was happening in that office which, day after day, was becoming the wall between us.

After the stock-market crash, I felt I was losing him completely. I hardly saw him at all. He spent his days shut in his office and often worked well past three in the morning. At night, the incessant beeping of the screens regularly rang through the house, signaling threshold breaches, alerts, market movements.

One night, one of those alert sounds burst so abruptly into the silence that I woke with a start, my heart racing wildly, with the genuine sensation of having a heart attack. I asked him never to bring his phone into the bedroom again. But what shook me most was not the noise. It was his reaction. Not a word. No apology. No sign of regret or concern. Only a cold, almost absent silence that ended with his return to his office.

In that instant, I genuinely wondered who he had become.

My nightmares had come back. I kept seeing that office plunged into a kind of thick fog, as if something dark were slowly growing inside it. His attitude no longer reassured me. I asked him to stop trading, but the subject had become a source of extreme tension between us. Deep down, I was convinced that this activity was leading him to his ruin. What I did not yet know was how far that fall would drag us both.

A few months later, his motivation had returned. For him, COVID had been only a "black swan": an exceptional, unpredictable event, a historical anomaly that did not really call his vision of the markets into question. He remained convinced that this crash belonged to a unique category of crisis, one not likely to recur anytime soon.

This conviction reinforced another belief very present at the time among many traders: that the cryptocurrency market obeyed rules different from those of traditional finance. Bitcoin and the other crypto-assets were seen as assets decorrelated from classic markets, capable of withstanding stock-market crises and the failures of the global financial system.

The idea seemed almost logical: if equity markets collapsed under the effect of a global health crisis, cryptocurrencies could continue on their own trajectory, independent of the economic and monetary chaos. Many saw in them the foundations of a new financial order.

But the spring of 2020 revealed a far more brutal reality. In periods of extreme fear, almost everything ends up becoming correlated. Investors sell in a hurry, seek liquidity, and liquidate even the assets they had until then considered protections. Cryptocurrencies too were swept up in the violence of the movement.

Yet, despite this shock, he continued to believe that the crisis was more of an exception than a genuine warning signal.

It is almost troubling to see how quickly a human being can recover from an immense fall by convincing himself that the worst already belongs to the past. A few months earlier, the markets were collapsing in panic. And yet, gradually, the fear faded. The "black swan" was relegated to oblivion and the euphoria returned with an almost unreal force.

This time, he was certain he had found the right strategy. A method he considered almost unbeatable. I remember the energy that filled him in that period. He spoke with a new, almost exalted confidence. He tried to explain his discovery to me, but without ever going into the technical details. All I understood was that the simulations run on past data produced exceptional performance. The figures seemed to confirm that the system worked.

But something in me remained uneasy. I asked him to be careful. I kept telling him that the markets had precisely this ability to give the illusion of control just before reminding you of their violence. At one point, my worry became such that I even asked his mother to try to reason with him.

Meanwhile, friends, relatives, people in our circle had begun to invest through him. And, on the surface, everything seemed to work. The returns were paid out regularly. The payments arrived on time. Each positive result reinforced the others' confidence even more... but also his own.

So, since everything seemed to work, I too ended up convincing myself that I had to support him to the end. After all, the results were there, the repayments continued, and the dominant idea was that this difficult period was only a temporary passage before a definitive return to balance.

I therefore decided to take out a loan in order to give him liquidity to repay certain debts and relieve the pressure that was beginning to build around him. In my mind, this was nothing reckless. I was convinced that within only a few months, the situation would be restored and we would easily repay this money.

But one detail troubled me deeply. Contrary to what I imagined, he did not want me to take out this loan. His attitude was strange, almost contradictory. He, who was constantly looking for financial solutions, suddenly seemed to refuse help that could nonetheless give him some breathing room.

At the time, I did not understand the reason. I thought it was pride, or perhaps guilt. I was far from imagining the truth. If he did not want me to borrow, it was not to protect me. It was because he already knew that the trading had become a catastrophe he was still striving to conceal hermetically.

It was, clearly, the biggest financial mistake of my life. He promised to honor the monthly installments. But after three months, when I insisted on getting proof of payment, his answer was curt:

> *"Don't you trust me? Can you change your tone when you speak to me?"*

The substance of the question disappeared beneath its form. I obtained no evidence. The only evidence that followed in the coming days was an implacable silence and a total absence of truth.

> *"It's going to be fine."*
>
> *"The market will come back up."*
>
> *"It's temporary."*
>
> *"In a week, we're good."*
>
> *"In a month, everything will be in order."*
>
> *"One more month."*

At that stage, I was in a state of almost total distress. This nightmare had been going on for nearly a year. An entire year spent living in the expectation of a return to normal that never came. I was tossed from one explanation to another, from one promise to the next, without ever having concrete proof, without real visibility, without any certainty to hold on to.

And yet, despite the inconsistencies, despite the anguish growing in me, I kept wanting to believe his answers. Like many women progressively locked into a relationship where opacity settles in through small, almost invisible layers, I still preferred to believe the words rather than to look reality fully in the face.

Because deep down, looking would have meant accepting something far more terrifying still: that the man to whom I had entrusted part of our security, our stability, and our future might already be in control of nothing at all.

* * *

The night everything tipped over

A few days before the final collapse, something changed abruptly in him. His behavior became unstable, unpredictable, almost foreign. As if an invisible tension had finally cracked what little control remained.

I remember deciding to visit a friend who was going through a difficult time. A simple decision, banal even. Yet his reaction was disproportionately violent. He suddenly flew into a rage, reproaching me for always running for others when it was he who needed me. His anger seemed to come from much further away than this simple visit. I did not understand what was really at play, but I left anyway.

The next day, my body gave way in turn. A brutal fever pinned me to the bed for several days. I was exhausted, unable to distinguish clearly what came from illness, from anguish, or from the fatigue accumulated over months.

And then there was this strange detail. He, who usually lived shut away in his office, almost absent from the house despite his physical presence, suddenly began making incessant back-and-forth trips into my room. As if he were agitated by something I could not yet see. As if he were trying, in a rush, to repair something that was already completely slipping away from him.

One evening, he came into the room with a silver ring in hand, to replace the one I had lost some time earlier. The gesture could have been tender. But in the state I was in, it provoked in me an immediate, almost instinctive anger. Despite the fever, I reproached him for always deciding alone, always acting without waiting, without sharing, without building with me. Why did he always have to choose, buy, repair alone? Why had we become two people living side by side without ever truly meeting?

And then, he suddenly took on a deeply crestfallen look.

I had never seen him like that. He knelt down beside my bed. His voice was barely audible, his face of an extreme gravity.

> *"I've lost everything."*

I did not understand. What? Everything what? What are you talking about?

> *"Everything. Absolutely everything. The fund. The investments. Your money. Everything."*

The silence that followed was unreal. Dense. Crushing. As if time itself had just been suspended in that room.

I was still trying to understand what he had just said. My mind refused to assemble the words together. Then, in just a few seconds, reality imposed itself with an indescribable violence.

Everything had vanished.

Instinctively I brought both hands to my mouth. I was trembling. My gaze searched for something to cling to in the room, anything that might still seem normal. But there was nothing normal anymore. The fever burned my body, my heart beat so hard that I felt it would explode. Then something gave way in me.

In a gesture of despair I would never have believed myself capable of, I began to hit him. With all my strength. As if my body were trying to expel entire years of fear, of lies, of confusion, and of betrayal accumulated in silence. I was crying. I was screaming. Nothing was controlled anymore.

And meanwhile, somewhere in the apartment, there were our children.

I still remember the strange silence that reigned that evening. As if they too had sensed, without truly understanding, that something irreversible had just broken within the walls of that house.

After the confession, something went out in the room. Perhaps even in him. Perhaps in me too.

For a few moments, I thought I saw a form of lucidity appear. As if the real weight of what had just been destroyed finally crossed his gaze. There was a brief, almost imperceptible crack, where I thought I recognized fear, regret, perhaps even an awareness. But it lasted only an instant.

Very quickly, he closed himself off completely. His face became strangely calm again. Almost impassive. And he looked at me with a distance so disturbing that, for a few seconds, I had the absurd impression that it was I who was losing my grip on reality. As if the collapse I was discovering became more difficult for him to bear in my gaze than in the concrete consequences he had nonetheless just caused.

And that is probably what destroyed me the most.

Not only the money that had vanished. Not only the losses. But that vertiginous sensation of being suddenly alone before the magnitude of the catastrophe. Alone in measuring what it really meant. Alone in watching the children, the house, the years built, the entire future waver all at once.

After that confession, there was almost no remorse expressed. Almost no visible emotion. As if he had had to cut himself off internally from the gravity of the consequences in order to keep moving forward without collapsing himself. As if fully acknowledging what this fall was doing to his family, to his children, to me, would have been psychically impossible to bear.

He belonged to that category of people who, confronted with a collapse too violent for their own mind, enter a form of deep emotional withdrawal. Not always out of conscious coldness or a total absence of love, but because looking the damage in the face would also mean confronting a guilt that had become unbearable. He never came out of it.

But at that moment, I did not yet see that. I simply saw a man who had just tipped us into a nameless horror... and who already seemed elsewhere.

It is that absence that devastated me the most. Not the figures. The absence.

***

After

That night, we did not eat. I protected the children by revealing nothing to them.

The next morning, on waking, I saw that fog again. But this time, it was no longer in his nightmares nor around that office I had so often imagined. It was there, in my own bedroom, suspended in the air like a silent and oppressive presence. For a few seconds, I sincerely believed I was losing my mind.

I had cried all night. One of those nights when the body ends up no longer distinguishing fatigue, fear, and grief. And yet, in the middle of that collapse, my thoughts hardly went toward myself. They went toward all those who had trusted him. Those who had invested through him. Those who did not yet know that their money had vanished.

And deep down, a certainty was beginning to impose itself with absolute brutality: the lie could not continue. The others had to be warned. This fall had to be stopped before it carried away even more lives with it.

Anger quickly gave way to a mixture of compassion and responsibility. I saw a man collapsing psychologically. A father. My husband. Someone I had loved.

So I did what I had always known how to do: try to repair what was falling apart. I put at his disposal everything I still had left. My savings. My energy. My support. A part of me still believed we could recover from this catastrophe. That, despite the magnitude of the disaster, there was still a possible way back.

But the very next morning, something had changed in me. At first light, I summoned all the loved ones who had invested through him. I could no longer bear the idea that the silence would continue while everything had already collapsed. And there, a truth chilled me: many had already been waiting for news from him for a long time, without success. The calls went unanswered. The messages too. Some were beginning to worry seriously, without yet imagining the real magnitude of the situation.

That morning, watching them come in one by one, I understood that the collapse no longer concerned only him and me. The fall had become collective.

And, for the first time, I thought of all those women who, before me, had brutally discovered that they lived beside a man whose inner world had progressively been built in secrecy, denial, and headlong flight. I thought of the wives of men like Bernie Madoff. For a long time, I had looked at that kind of story from a distance, almost the way one watches a financial scandal on television: figures, frauds, the guilty, the victims. But that morning, I suddenly understood that at the heart of these affairs there were also entire families caught in a psychological collapse impossible to describe.

Because when a man drags others into his fall, the woman who shares his life does not lose only money. She loses her bearings. Her perception of reality. Her confidence in her own judgment. She revisits every memory, every silence, every absence, every inconsistency, asking herself: "How could I not have seen?"

And the most terrible part is perhaps right there. You discover that for months — sometimes years — two realities have coexisted under the same roof. The one you thought you were living. And the one the other was desperately trying to keep standing despite his inner collapse.

I suddenly understood that the real trauma did not come only from the financial losses. It came also from that deep psychological fracture: realizing that the man with whom you shared your life was waging, in silence, a battle that even love, closeness, and the shared years had not been enough to make visible.

But while, on my side, I was desperately trying to contain the collapse, he already seemed to be plunging back into the same mechanisms. While I was still looking for how to protect what could be protected, he kept investing. Worse still, he kept making other people in his circle invest.

The same promises. The same strategies presented as rational. The same behaviors that had nonetheless already destroyed our own financial stability.

Something became clear to me at that moment: the full psychological power of this kind of fall. When a person sinks far enough into the spiral of losses, acknowledging reality sometimes becomes even more unbearable than continuing to take risks. As if each new investment absolutely had to become the one that would repair everything. The one that would erase the previous mistakes, repay, restore the self-image, make the shame disappear.

But in reality, the further he went, the wider the chasm grew.

That is where something broke definitively in me.

A few weeks after the night everything had collapsed, we left for the south of France. Officially, it was a family trip. In reality, it was something else. A slow crossing through the rubble. My brother's family wanted to understand. To understand how such a fall had been possible. To understand at what moment everything had escaped us. Above all, to understand how a chasm so immense could have grown for so long in silence.

I remember that week as a suspended, unreal time, almost without light. The days seemed long, stifling, and the nights even more so. For seven days, I barely slept. Not really. My body stayed lying down, but my mind kept falling.

I carried it all.

The shame.

The shame of seeing our family exposed to something so violent.

The pain of those who had lost their savings by trusting him.

The looks laden with questions to which I myself had no answer.

The heavy silences around the tables.

The contained anger of loved ones who had asked for nothing and yet found themselves dragged into our fall.

And above all of this, there was that fear. A physical fear. Primal. Almost animal.

The fear that he would not bear the weight of what he had done.

The fear that he would disappear.

The chasm had become so abyssal that this thought kept returning to my mind, in spite of myself. I looked at my children and wondered how to still protect something of their innocence in the middle of such chaos.

And while I carried the looks, the questions, the consequences, while my heart pounded day and night under the effect of anguish and guilt, he slept.

He reasoned.

Calmly. Methodically.

He held forth in a structured, almost technical discourse about market risks, volatility, cycles, exceptional events. As if all of this still belonged to a simple economic demonstration. As if this catastrophe could be contained within charts, probabilities, and rational explanations.

But in that room, there were no markets. There were faces. Families. The savings of years of work. People who had trusted.

And yet, no regret seemed to truly cross his words. He analyzed. He justified. He explained. But he acknowledged neither the lies, nor the silence, nor the fact of having dragged his own family into such danger. More troubling still: he did not even seem to understand what he was actually being reproached for.

Because what we reproached him for was not only the financial loss.

Markets can fall. Money can be lost. Anyone who invests knows this reality. But what had destroyed something far deeper was the opacity. The concealments. The repeated promises while everything was already collapsing. The fact of having continued to drag others into a fall he probably knew about well before we did.

It was not only a financial bankruptcy. It was a breach of trust so deep that it seemed to have fractured even our shared perception of reality.

Money that is lost can be understood. Financial mistakes too. The markets have always had the power to destroy in a few weeks what years had taken to build.

But what seemed unbearable to me was not only the fall. It was the silence that had preceded it. The years of concealment. The fact of never having found the strength to tell the truth to the woman who shared his bed, raised his children, and built her life by his side.

With hindsight, I believe he could no longer face that truth himself. Not necessarily out of conscious cruelty, but because fully admitting what was happening would have meant looking the consequences of his actions on those he loved straight in the face.

So he took refuge in analysis. The figures. The technical reasoning. The market mechanisms. Where everything could still seem abstract, almost impersonal. Where there were no wounded gazes, no sleepless nights, no fear slowly eating away at an entire family.

Meanwhile, I contained the human impact of the catastrophe. The fear. The shame. The tensions. The anguish of others. The children's future. I took upon myself what he seemed incapable of facing emotionally.

And this image stays etched in me: him, sleeping, while I lay awake staring at the ceiling until morning.

That is when I understood something essential: we no longer lived the same inner reality. For a long time already, I had been carrying an emotional burden that was not entirely mine. I supported, I protected, I absorbed, believing that this was simply part of love.

And in a way, yes, it was love.

But love cannot durably survive when a single person carries the psychological, moral, and emotional weight of two lives. That imbalance always ends up breaking something.

In the weeks that followed, I finally demanded all the documents I had been asking for for months. Nothing could remain in the fog any longer. I needed to see. To understand. Even if each answer now seemed capable of destroying me a little more.

And the more the documents arrived, the darker the reality became. The amounts committed in my name far exceeded what I had imagined. Each statement, each figure, each detail discovered opened a new chasm beneath my feet. I sometimes had the impression that the catastrophe kept pushing back its own limits, as if the bottom no longer existed.

That is undoubtedly the essential difference between the moment when one discovers a betrayal and the moment when one truly measures its full extent.

The first breaks you.

The second forces you to survive.

And in that face-to-face with reality, I understood something that would never be said aloud around a family table, nor in the advice of well-meaning friends, nor even in the offices of specialized lawyers.

The man I had married no longer existed.

Perhaps he had never existed as I had believed him to be.

* * *

What this chapter reveals

He often repeated this line from Warren Buffett: "Only when the tide goes out do you discover who's been swimming naked." I did not yet grasp its full scope. Today, I believe it perfectly sums up what I went through.

As long as money keeps circulating, many fragilities remain invisible. Income compensates for mistakes, new inflows of money push back the consequences, and balances that are nonetheless unstable still manage to give the illusion of holding up. Even profoundly unbalanced systems can seem to function for a long time.

Then a major event arrives: a job loss, a stock-market crash, an illness, an inability to work, a global lockdown. And suddenly, everything collapses.

We then believe the crisis is the cause of the fall. But in reality, it is often only its brutal revealer. The moment when what was already cracked becomes impossible to hide. Because the real causes are almost always older, deeper, and more silent than the event that finally makes everything fall.

Financial violence in a couple does not lie only in the loss of money. It lies also in discovering, sometimes after years, that one has been kept at a distance from a reality that nonetheless fully committed one's future.

In a financial scandal, investors lose what they already own. But in some households, women also lose what they have not yet had time to build: their future, the years it will take to rebuild, the security of their children, and sometimes even the inner capacity to begin again one day without fear.

And it is precisely because this violence takes place in the intimacy of the couple that it is so difficult to identify. The space where one should be most protected sometimes becomes the one where one sees least clearly.

* * *

What this chapter teaches — rules and actions

Silent financial violence does not look like what we imagine. It begins with opacity, settles into trust, and reveals itself often too late. These rules are here so that it no longer goes unnoticed.

Rule 27. Repeated financial opacity is always a warning signal. Vague answers, documents never shown, questions that trigger conflicts rather than answers — these are not the signs of an overwhelmed partner. They are signals.

Rule 28. Participating in the financial decisions of your household is not a lack of trust. It is a responsibility. Understanding the accounts, knowing the debts, knowing what is invested — this is not controlling the other. It is being present in your own life.

Rule 29. Technical competence protects neither from denial, nor from ego, nor from risky behavior. Working in finance does not make someone immune to psychological biases. Overconfidence, the need to recover a loss, the refusal to stop — these are human mechanisms that affect experts too.

Rule 30. A single person should never carry alone the entire financial reality of a couple. It is too heavy a burden for one person — and too great a vulnerability for the other.

Action 1. The nine visibility questions. Anyone living in a couple should be able to answer these questions without hesitation: What is the household's real income? What debts currently exist? What investments are held, and in whose name? Are there products using leverage? What is the worst possible financial scenario? What genuinely available savings does the household have? What accounts exist, and who has access to them? What taxes or charges remain owed? If asking these questions systematically provokes aggression, guilt-tripping, or vagueness — the problem is no longer only financial.

No one will build your security for you.

PART VI

What I rebuilt

Chapter 9 — The brutal awakening

Forty years old, and everything to rebuild

I came back from the south of France on a Saturday, without knowing how one comes home when home no longer exists.

The children were asleep on the back seat. He was driving. And I, in the passenger seat, watched the landscapes go by, wondering how an entire life could fit into the silence of a car driving home.

For weeks, I remained a prisoner of the same questions. Why had he not stopped? Why had he told me nothing? Why continue when everything was already collapsing?

But there was no clear answer. Or perhaps there had never been one. And I understood something painful: sometimes, the absence of an answer destroys even more than the truth itself. Because it leaves you alone with your hypotheses, alone with your incomprehension, alone facing someone who even ends up looking at you as if the problem came from your questions rather than from his actions.

We often say that love is blind. It is true. But what is said less often is how difficult it is to open your eyes when an entire part of you still refuses to see. Because seeing then forces you to act. Seeing forces you to accept that the reality you were living in had perhaps not existed for a long time already.

And then, one day, something changed in me.

I stopped trying to fully understand why he had done all of this. That answer, I believe today, I will never completely have. By dint of looking at his fall, his lies, his mechanisms, I had ended up disappearing from the equation myself.

So, for the first time, my gaze shifted toward another question: what had been my own role in this story?

I had just turned forty. That age of which it is often said that it forces you to face your own truth. You finally look at your life without evasion. You gradually stop pushing away the questions you had buried under daily life, work, responsibilities, love, or fear. What still works? What is slowly destroying me? What do I never again want to accept?

And this time, reality had become impossible to sidestep.

I was living with someone who lied permanently. Not an occasional lie. Not an isolated mistake. But an entire system built on concealment, omissions, half-truths, and parallel realities. The lie had ended up becoming the invisible structure of our shared life.

And at that precise instant, something was set off in me with an almost brutal clarity. A form of lucidity I had never felt before.

Enough.

***

The moment of clarity

For my fortieth birthday, my friends organized a surprise trip to Paris for me. And, for the first time in a very long while, I felt something I had almost believed gone: joy. A simple joy. Calm. Without tension. There was also that strange sensation of inner peace, that forgotten lightness one no longer notices when one has lived too long in anguish.

In leaving, even for a few days, the heavy and silently oppressive atmosphere that my house had become, I suddenly became aware of something vertiginous: I had stopped being myself a long time ago.

I had lost myself progressively. Without noise. Without a visible rupture. The way some people drift slowly away from a shore without even feeling the current carry them off. And the most troubling part is that no one really seemed to have seen it. Not even me.

By dint of carrying the fears, the tensions, the crises, the silences, and the responsibilities of others, I had ended up disappearing behind a function: staying upright. Surviving. Repairing. Containing.

And, in Paris, amid the laughter of my friends, the lively streets, the simple conversations, and that almost unreal parenthesis, a thought crossed me with immense brutality: if I continued this way, in five years, there might be nothing left of the woman I had been.

I returned to Geneva.

And as soon as I crossed the threshold of the house, the anguish returned almost instantly. As if my body recognized, before I did, the atmosphere in which it had learned to survive for months. The air felt heavy. Familiar. Oppressive.

My family was waiting for me to blow out my birthday candles. There were smiles, voices, an attempt at normality suspended amid the invisible ruins of our life. Then I saw him.

The man who had driven our existence toward bankruptcy.

And in that instant, something in me stopped definitively.

There was no more compassion. No more sadness. Not even hope. Everything that had long resisted in me — the wish to understand, to save, to still repair — seemed to have gone out silently during that trip.

In its place remained something else.

A cold lucidity.

Calm.

Almost clinical.

And, for the first time in a very long while, a perfectly clear inner decision.

I was ready.

***

The confrontation

The next day, one last time, the part of me still conditioned to preserve the balance tried to obtain answers. Not new promises. Not new explanations. I simply wanted to access the elements still missing from the documents already provided. Some areas remained unclear. Some amounts did not add up. And the further I went, the more I felt that the essential was still hidden.

The tension rose immediately. As if each additional question became a threat. But this time, something had changed in me. I no longer backed down. I no longer tried to defuse the conflict to recover an artificial peace. I wanted to see reality to the very end, even if it had to destroy me.

He eventually shut himself in his office. And, for the first time, I followed him without giving in.

I still remember the oppressive silence of that room. The screens on. The cold light. His sudden agitation. He was trembling slightly. His sentences became confused. As if what he had managed to keep separate for months was finally beginning to collapse under its own weight.

After long minutes, he finally took out the missing documents.

The shock was immediate.

On discovering his true tax situation, I felt my body waver. My mind almost refused what my eyes were reading. I screamed. All the violence of the preceding months suddenly seemed to take a concrete, irreversible form, laid out before me on a few sheets of paper.

And yet, he remained almost impassive.

He looked at me with a troubling distance, as if my reaction were disproportionate. As if the problem lay more in my emotional collapse than in what had just been revealed.

And what shook me most that day was no longer even the figures themselves.

It was the absence of real emotion.

As if he were already internally cut off from the human consequences of his actions.

I called a friend. Not to resolve anything — there was nothing left to resolve in the immediate — but simply to hear a human voice capable of bringing me back to reality.

That evening, two certainties imposed themselves on me with absolute clarity. A confirmation of the day before.

If I stayed, I would end up losing myself entirely.

And he could probably never fully acknowledge his responsibility, because facing that truth would also have meant facing the image of himself that he was still desperately trying to preserve.

So, for the first time, leaving was no longer an abstract idea.

It had become a necessity.

***

The departure

Leaving the family home with my two children, I began to discover the real extent of the disaster.

The unpaid bills.

The debts accumulated in silence.

The financial commitments contracted without my truly grasping their existence.

It was like gradually entering the backstage of a parallel reality that had coexisted with my life for years without my truly seeing it. Each letter, each reminder, each administrative step revealed a new layer of what had been hidden.

Then I went to the tax office to begin the first procedures. And it was there that another truth struck me with a particular violence: I was jointly responsible.

Not because I had consciously made those decisions.

Not because I had wanted those debts.

But because I had lived alongside all of this without looking closely enough at what was really happening.

And that realization was probably one of the most difficult to accept.

Because in many couples, especially when the financial roles become unbalanced, the absence of oversight ends up becoming a form of invisible vulnerability. You think you are delegating. You think you are trusting. Until the day you discover that legally, administratively, and financially, the consequences exist despite your ignorance.

The truth did not reveal itself all at once. It imposed itself slowly, progressively, like water rising soundlessly until it ends up flooding everything.

Over the weeks, I understood that the losses did not date from yesterday. For years, he had been suffering significant, repeated, sometimes massive financial failures — without ever really telling me. During all that time, he had maintained around us an appearance of almost normal stability.

But behind that facade, everything rested on an extremely fragile balance.

The bills were concealed.

The delays accumulated.

The financial emergencies were shifted, postponed, disguised to buy a little more time.

And while reality was silently deteriorating, our life continued on the surface as if nothing really threatened to collapse.

How can one maintain an illusion with such constancy without ending up living inside it psychologically oneself? At what point does it cease to be only deception and become also a mental survival mechanism? As if, faced with losses that had become too heavy, some people progressively built a parallel reality allowing them to keep functioning without collapsing inside.

It was no longer only about hiding the truth from others. It was perhaps also about becoming incapable of inhabiting it fully oneself.

I found myself facing a chasm.

Behind me, a past in ruins.

Before me, a future suddenly impossible to read.

There was that debt I had not consciously contracted. That responsibility that had imposed itself on me without my really having chosen it. And despite the injustice, despite the stunned shock, one truth remained: I no longer had the luxury of collapsing.

I had to get back up.

To survive.

To protect my children.

And perhaps also to find again, somewhere beneath the rubble, the woman I had stopped being.

* * *

What many women ignore — joint tax liability in Switzerland

In Switzerland, married spouses are jointly liable for the household's income and wealth tax — even if one of them had no knowledge of the declared income or assets. This joint liability means the tax authority can claim the entire debt from either spouse, regardless of who made the financial decisions. After a separation, it is possible to request separate taxation — but this step must be actively initiated. It is not automatic. In case of doubt, contact the cantonal tax service or consult a lawyer specialized in tax law.

The phases

I went through, one by one, all the phases that those who discover a betrayal of this magnitude go through.

First, compassion. Because when you have deeply loved someone, the first reflex is not always to protect yourself. It is often to want to save the other despite what he has destroyed.

Then the anger arrived. A deep, violent, almost physical anger. Not only against the losses or the lies, but against those entire years during which reality had been concealed before my eyes.

Then came depression. That moment when the truth ceases to be information and becomes a permanent state. Reality was there, brutal, undeniable, impossible to sidestep.

Then shame.

That silent question that gnaws at you: how could I not have seen? How could I have let such a situation grow for so long without stopping it?

And finally, guilt. The heaviest of all. Because it forced me to look at a question I did not want to hear: what had been my own role in this story?

Trusting your partner should be something natural. It is even one of the most essential foundations of a life built together.

And yet, at the same time, I was discovering that having given blind trust had made me extremely vulnerable.

These two truths now coexisted in me, uncomfortable, almost contradictory, without either really managing to erase the other.

The American psychologist Elisabeth Kübler-Ross described the five stages of grief — denial, anger, bargaining, depression, acceptance — from the experience of people facing death. Later research showed that these same stages apply to any major loss: a relationship, an identity, a security one believed acquired. I went through them all. Not in order. Sometimes several at once. Sometimes going backward.

What finally began to free me from this cycle was when I stopped looking only at his acts and turned my gaze at last toward my own mechanisms, my silences, and everything I had accepted in the name of love, of trust, or of the fear of seeing reality.

Not his fault. My part.

I had absented myself from the equation. Not out of negligence. Out of conditioning. Out of misplaced trust. Out of models integrated since childhood that I had never questioned. A couple does not function one-way — the decisions of one affect the other, always. And I had let myself be carried along.

I am convinced he did not set out with bad intentions. He believed in his strategies. But he was losing. Again and again. Without ever adapting. Without ever stopping. Without ever telling the truth.

There is a dimension there that I took time to name: emotional disconnection from money. The closer one is to the markets, the more one can detach from what money really represents — the sacrifices, the years of work, the lives built behind every franc. When that empathy disappears, managing other people's money becomes dangerous. One can lose everything without stopping, without measuring, without protecting.

But it is precisely by acknowledging my own part that I found again something essential: a lever. I was no longer only the victim of a situation. I was also someone who had let that situation exist.

And someone who let it happen can also decide to stop letting it happen.

That is where it all began. The deconstruction.

* * *

What this chapter teaches — rules and actions

This chapter is not only the account of a fall. It is the moment when awareness becomes irreversible. Here is what it teaches — and what you can do right now.

Rule 31. Joint tax liability exists even without a conscious signature. In Switzerland, spouses are jointly liable for the household's taxes. If your partner hides debts or income, you can be held responsible. Ignorance does not protect you before the tax authority.

Rule 32. Trusting is not delegating. Trusting someone means believing in them. Delegating without looking means transferring a responsibility to them without a safeguard. These two things are profoundly different. You can love someone and still ask to see the accounts.

Rule 33. Emotional disconnection from money is a warning signal. Someone who no longer feels the weight of what they are risking — who invests other people's money without empathy for what that money represents — is dangerous to entrust shared resources to. It is not a question of competence. It is a question of psychology.

Rule 34. Acknowledging your part is not punishing yourself. It is recovering your power. As long as you identify only as a victim, you remain passive. The day you ask yourself "what could I have done differently?" — that day, you find a lever again.

Action 1. Ask for a copy of your last joint tax return. Read it. If you do not understand what is in it, call your canton's tax service — they are required to explain it to you. This step takes an hour. It can prevent years of consequences.

Action 2. If you are in the process of separating, or considering it, consult a lawyer specialized in family law before signing anything. In Switzerland, the liquidation of the matrimonial regime, the division of the second pillar, and joint debts follow precise rules. Not knowing them can cost you years of rebuilding.

Action 3. Make a list of everything you do not know about your shared finances. Not to accuse — to see. Joint bank accounts, mortgages, insurance policies, second and third pillars, possible debts. If you cannot answer these questions on your own, you are absent from your own financial security.

Action 4. If you are going through a difficult separation, seek support on three levels simultaneously: legal, financial, and psychological. The three are linked. A decision made under emotional shock can have lasting financial consequences. Stabilize yourself before signing definitive commitments.

Chapter 10 — The two costumes

What my profession could not do for me

A question stayed with me throughout this crossing. A question I did not dare formulate aloud, because it contained something too painful to look at. How could this have happened to me?

There is a question that haunted me for a long time. A question I did not dare formulate aloud, because it contained something too painful to look at in the face.

How could this have happened to me?

Not to me in the sense of someone chosen, a woman superior to others. But to me — the one who worked in finance. The one who analyzed risk. The one whose profession consisted precisely in protecting investors from this kind of situation.

My entire career had been built around these questions. I had started in financial audit before progressively moving toward wealth management, then toward functions linked to risk and investor protection. This path is no coincidence, I understand now. I had chosen useful work. Work that protects. Work in which vigilance, questioning, and verification are reflexes — not options.

And yet, at home, I had stopped questioning. I had stopped verifying. I had let exactly the gray areas settle in that my profession taught me to detect.

***

The two costumes

At the office, I was trained to detect risk. I analyzed. I questioned. I checked. I verified. It had become a professional reflex, almost second nature.

But coming home, I took off that costume to put on another.

I became a wife. A mother. A woman who simply wanted to love, build, trust.

These two women coexisted in me without ever really speaking to each other. The professional and the wife. The analyst and the woman in love. The one who knew. And the one whose intuitions, ideas, and worries always ended up being stifled once the door of the house had closed.

And yet, at times, I felt these two parts of me come together.
I remember certain conversations with him, where something in me was still trying to bring lucidity into the middle of the chaos. I reminded him of principles I knew deeply: that no investment is truly without risk, that transparency toward the people who entrust their money is not an option but a responsibility, and that concealed losses almost always end up resurfacing one way or another.

On the surface, these discussions stayed general, almost theoretical. But in reality, they were deeply personal.

Especially when he began wanting to invest in assets then operating in a still very lightly regulated environment, where the absence of framework, control, and supervision sometimes left as much room for opportunities as for excesses.

I was not heard.

Was it a legitimacy bias? The fact that in his eyes I was first his wife before being a professional capable of analyzing certain risks with lucidity?

Or perhaps something even more deeply rooted: that silent reality found in some couples, where a woman's economic voice ends up carrying less weight, even when she possesses the skills, the experience, or the intuition needed to see what the other still refuses to look at.

I still cannot fully answer this question. But it continues to work on me.

* * *

What research says about expert women within their couples

Studies in social psychology reveal a phenomenon called "invisible competence": women whose professional expertise is recognized outside the home frequently see that same expertise undervalued in their domestic environment. Their technical word is received differently depending on the context — not because they are less competent, but because the spousal or maternal role activates perception biases that minimize their authority on subjects that are nonetheless within their field. This phenomenon is documented in heterosexual couples but also in some broader family structures.

The lifeline

When everything collapsed at home, my work became a lifeline.

Crossing through the doors each morning, I could almost forget what awaited me when I got home. Not really forget — but suspend. Put on pause a reality too heavy to be carried continuously. At the office, I functioned. I delivered. I thought clearly. It was, paradoxically, the place where I was most myself.

And I had the immense good fortune to be surrounded by a humanity I will never forget.

My manager at the time played a role I only fully understood much later. At a moment when everything was collapsing inside, when the very idea of continuing to work seemed impossible to me, I was seriously considering going on full medical leave.

It was then that he said something to me that I did not immediately understand, but whose rightness became clear to me over time:

> *"Absolutely not. Today more than ever, you need to keep a cool head."*

He was trying, no doubt, to preserve something in me that I could no longer see myself: my lucidity.

Because he had understood — perhaps before I did — that what would allow me to get through this period was not only rest, but the ability to keep a connection to a form of structure, of clarity, of outside reality.

And that a total stop, in the psychological state I was in then, might risk leaving all the room to inner chaos.

There were also other moments. Instants tiny in appearance, but which stay etched because they reveal what is most human in others when our own world collapses.

One morning, I arrived at the office completely shaken. I could no longer contain what was happening inside me. I shut myself alone in a meeting room, trying to regain control, to breathe normally, to act as if everything could still hold together a few hours longer.

Then a colleague came in quietly. He looked at me for a few seconds, without insisting, without asking useless questions. And he simply said:

> *"If you need time, go. We've got it covered."*

That sentence made me break down immediately.

Not because it was spectacular or dramatic. But precisely because it was not. It contained something deeply human: presence, silent solidarity, that rare way of supporting someone without trying to invade their pain.

I started crying even harder. Then I went out and walked for nearly an hour around my workplace, trying to find a little air, a little calm, a little coherence in the middle of what was destroying my life.

We often hear that one must know how to separate private life from professional life. To maintain a clear boundary. To keep functioning, producing, moving forward, as if the inner storms could always stay at the office door.

But there are moments in a life when that boundary ends up cracking despite us. Moments when the pain, the exhaustion, or the shock become too great to stay perfectly contained behind a controlled appearance.

And that day, I understood that before the functions, the titles, or the professional roles, there were simply human beings.

And that, sometimes, in the darkest periods, humanity surges precisely where we no longer expected it.

* * *

The expert's guilt

For a long time, I reproached myself for one precise thing. Not for having trusted — trust is not a fault. But for not having applied at home what I applied everywhere else.

You work in risk. In investor protection. And you did not see what was happening in your own home.

This thought kept returning. Relentlessly. Like a silent condemnation I pronounced against my own person.

But this period taught me something essential, something that neither professional training nor years of experience had taught me: skills do not automatically protect us when affect, love, trust, and the dynamic of the couple come into play.

Technical knowledge is not enough. It must be accompanied by presence — by an active will to look, to question, to refuse the gray areas. Even when it disturbs. Even when it creates conflict. Even when the relationship seems to pay for it.

Because silence protects peace in the short term. It destroys security in the long term.

***

There are no more costumes

This ordeal transformed me in a way I would not have chosen but that I do not regret.

Today, there are no longer two versions of myself. No longer the professional on one side and the woman of the home on the other. No more costumes to put on depending on where I find myself.

I am the same woman everywhere.

The rigor I apply in my profession, I have learned to apply also to my own life. The questions I professionally ask others, I now ask of myself. And the vigilance I exercise to protect investors' savings, I exercise today with the same demand to protect my own.

This coherence is priceless.

Of course, a part of me sometimes thinks that if I had had this lucidity earlier, I would have spared myself much suffering. But I cannot deny what this crossing taught me about the human, about risk, about trust, about vulnerability. My understanding of these mechanisms today far exceeds what years of professional expertise had given me alone.

* * *

The human, always

There is another dimension of this story that I never really knew how to tell.

Over time, I came to understand that beyond the financial mistakes, there probably existed a much deeper psychological suffering in the father of my children. Losing a lot of money can tip some people into irrational behaviors: shame, denial, the fear of failure, the obsession with recovering, the will to hide losses to preserve an image. In that spiral, decisions become more and more destructive — not out of malice, but out of an inability to get out of the dynamic.

You cannot help someone who refuses to acknowledge their own suffering.

Money has taken such a central place in our societies that some would be ready to do anything to avoid losing, to avoid falling, to avoid being seen differently. And in that race, we sometimes forget the essential.

The human. Always the human.

And even today, I cannot help thinking this: if he had simply had confidence in me — if he had had the courage to speak to me with transparency, with honesty, with the lucidity that true love demands — I am almost certain that we would have found a solution together.

This certainty has not reconciled me with what happened. But it has reconciled me with him, as a fallible human being. And perhaps, deep down, with myself.

* * *

What this chapter teaches

Professional competence does not automatically protect in personal life. It is one of the most difficult truths to accept — and one of the most liberating once you have integrated it.

Rule 35. Technical knowledge is not enough without active presence. Knowing is not looking. You can know all the mechanisms of financial risk and choose, consciously or not, not to apply them to your own life. Vigilance must be a daily decision — not only a professional skill.

Rule 36. A woman's legitimacy does not stop at the door of her home. If your technical word is ignored in your couple because you are first perceived as a wife or a mother, that is an imbalance to name. Not to accept.

Rule 37. Being the same person everywhere is a strength, not a lack of flexibility. The coherence between the woman one is at work and the woman one is at home is not rigidity — it is integrity. And that integrity is a form of protection no one can take away.

Action 1. Identify a financial decision in your personal life that you would never have accepted in a professional setting. A contract not read. A signature made in a rush. An investment whose mechanisms you do not understand.

That gap between what you demand at the office and what you accept at home is precisely where the work begins.

Action 2. The next time you feel uneasy about a financial decision in your couple — a figure that does not add up, an answer too vague, an artificial urgency — apply the professional reflex: ask to see the documents. Ask the questions. Take your time. You have the right to be as demanding for yourself as for any client.

Chapter 11 — The deconstruction

Order, disorder, reorder

We imagine reconstruction as a project — a staircase one climbs one step at a time. The reality looks more like moving house after a fire. You do not yet know what you are keeping.

The awakening was brutal. Violent. Destabilizing. I could compare it to birth — that instant when a being leaves the water, the silence, and the protection to abruptly discover air, light, and cold. It is a physical shock as much as an existential one. I had come out of a world I thought I controlled to discover that I knew nothing. That I had managed nothing. Not the taxes. Not the paperwork. Not the financial decisions. Everything had been in his hands. And that had suited me — until the day everything collapsed.

Deconstructing took three years. Because there are stages one cannot skip. First, you accuse. You give the other all the responsibility. And as long as you accuse, you do not see yourself. Then comes the moment when you turn back toward yourself. Truly. And when you accept to see your part. Finally, you rebuild. Order. Disorder. Reorder. The disorder is violent. But it is necessary. It is in that chaos that clarity is born.

***

Looking the iceberg in the face

The first step was the most dreaded: assessing the damage.

Within a few days, I received dozens of reminder letters from the tax authority — addressed to my name, for the first time, because I had never existed in this correspondence before. The amounts included penalties of several thousand francs, accumulated over years of fruitless reminders. It was up to me to pay my share.

I put all those letters in a bag. And I carried that bag around for days, without finding the courage to open it. I was paralyzed. Frozen by a fear I had never known — that of looking in the face at a reality I had not created but for which I was now responsible.

I could not do it alone.

A friend came. One afternoon, he laid the letters on the table and opened them one by one, while I struggled not to collapse. He sorted them in order of severity. Then he simply told me: start by repaying what costs you the most — the highest penalties — then work your way toward the rest.

How was I going to manage? I had transferred all my savings to my ex-partner to help him get back up. There was nothing left.

Without another word, this friend paid seventy percent of the first debt left by my partner in my name.

The shock was immense. Why? He answered me:

"If money isn't for this, then it's for nothing."

I want to pay tribute to this act here, because it went beyond simple generosity. It showed me, concretely, that money can be a tool of solidarity — not only of personal construction. And above all, it gave me something invaluable: the possibility of starting over.

I followed his advice. Over the two years that followed, I repaid methodically — the small debts first, then the larger ones. One franc after another.

***

Educating oneself in order to rebuild

Alongside the repayment, I began a work of self-assessment I had never done. Identifying my biases. Naming my conditioning. Understanding why I had delegated for so long without looking.

I read. A lot. Books on personal finance, on the psychology of money, on financial behaviors. What struck me most was the ease with which I understood notions that had seemed inaccessible to me before. Finance was not impenetrable. It had simply been presented to me as such — or rather, no one had ever presented it to me at all.

Financial education is not an expert's knowledge. It is a knowledge of life. And its absence does not protect — it exposes.

A few books that helped me rebuild

The Psychology of Money by Morgan Housel — to understand that our financial behaviors are above all human, not rational. Rich Dad Poor Dad by Robert Kiyosaki — to grasp the distinction between assets and liabilities, and why what you own matters as much as what you earn. The Millionaire Next Door by Thomas Stanley — to understand that real wealth is invisible and is built over time. These readings do not replace a financial advisor. But they give a language, a framework, and above all an inner permission to take an interest.

I also worked on forgiveness. Because I needed to forgive myself. To forgive myself for not having looked. For not having asked. For not having insisted when my intuition was telling me something was wrong. And to forgive — not forget, not excuse, but set down — so as not to remain a prisoner of what had happened.

I had a therapist accompany me. This inner work was as important as the financial work. The two are linked. You do not rebuild your financial life without rebuilding, at the same time, the relationship with yourself.

***

Rebuilding in the right order

Then came the moment of concrete action. But I learned something essential: you do not begin by investing. You begin by cleaning up.

Looking your finances in the face. Understanding your debts. Identifying the hidden commitments. Budgeting. Repaying. Cleaning up. It is in that order that reconstruction is possible — and in no other.

Many debts are invisible traps. We look at what we receive — the salary, the income — without looking at what we will have to give back. The interest. The penalties. The real cost of a consumer loan, a lease, an unregularized overdraft. What we do not measure always ends up catching up with us.

The real cost we never look at

A consumer loan of 10,000 francs repaid over 48 months at a rate of 10% actually costs more than 12,000 francs. An unregularized bank overdraft can reach rates of 12 to 15% per year. A tax debt with late penalties can double in a few years. These figures are not here to frighten — they are here to make visible what the financial system has an interest in keeping invisible. Understanding the real cost of your debts is the first act of a serious reconstruction.

It is only after cleaning up that one can consider building. And even at that stage, one must stay humble. Financial markets are not a playground. They are a place where one takes calculated risks — and where those who do not understand what they are doing can lose everything. Again.

* * *

Freedom without knowledge is a fragility

What this period taught me goes beyond my own story.

For decades, women fought for their rights, for their freedom, for equality. These struggles were necessary and legitimate. But in that conquest, something essential was often left aside: financial education. We obtained the right to work, to open an account, to invest, to own — without anyone teaching us to do any of it.

Freedom without knowledge is a door open onto a void.

The philosopher and feminist activist bell hooks wrote that the emancipation of women could not be limited to access to formal rights — it had to include the concrete tools to exercise those rights. Financial education is one of those tools. Perhaps the most fundamental, because it conditions all the others.

When a system of oppression collapses, the freedom obtained must be accompanied by a work of reconstruction, of learning, of reappropriation. Without this, the old patterns persist — not out of ill will, but because consciousness does not transform overnight. It is inherited. It is shaped. It demands active work to be changed.

That is what I did. And that is what this book proposes we do together.

Today, I no longer separate my professional life from my personal life. What I learn, I apply. What I understand, I pass on. To know in order to decide —

it is around this simple but fundamental idea that my entire reconstruction was articulated.

* * *

What this chapter teaches — rules and actions

Deconstruction is not a punishment. It is a process. Here is how to go through it in the right order.

Rule 38. You do not rebuild on a debt you have not looked at. The first step is not to invest — it is to inventory. All the debts, all the commitments, all the running interest. What you do not see keeps running.

Rule 39. The order of reconstruction is fixed: assessment → debt clearance → precautionary savings → investment. Skipping a step means building on sand.

Rule 40. Financial education is not reserved for experts. It is accessible to anyone willing to devote a few hours a week to it. What is missing is not capacity — it is exposure.

Rule 41. Forgiveness is part of financial reconstruction. Remaining in accusation — toward the other or toward yourself — consumes energy that should go toward action. You can acknowledge what happened without staying locked inside it.

Rule 42. Surrounding yourself is not a weakness. It is a strategy. A friend, an advisor, a therapist, a community — no one rebuilds alone, and those who claim to have done so have simply forgotten who helped them.

Action 1. Do your complete financial assessment this month. On one sheet, list: all your accounts and their balances, all your debts with their amount, their interest rate, and their due date, all your regular commitments. This is your real starting point — not the one you imagine.

Action 2. Sort your debts by real cost, not by amount. A debt of 2,000 francs at 18% interest costs more than a debt of 10,000 francs at 2%. Repay first what costs you the most per month. It is mathematical.

Action 3. Build a budget in four blocks in this order: fixed charges (rent, insurance, subscriptions) / debt repayment / precautionary savings — target: three months of charges / current living expenses. No investment as long as the first two blocks are not stable.

Action 4. Devote one hour a week to your financial education. A book, a podcast, a serious article. In six months, you will have enough understanding to make your own decisions. The recommended resources are at the end of the book.

Action 5. If you are going through a reconstruction after a separation, seek support on three levels simultaneously: legal, financial, and psychological. The three are linked. Treating one without the others slows everything down.

Chapter 12 — Taking back the power

The first free decisions

Deconstruction takes away. Taking back the power, on the other hand, demands that you build — with what remains, under the conditions that are mine now, no longer waiting for the perfect conditions that never came.

There is an image that often comes back to me when I think about that period: the chrysalis.

We generally imagine the transformation of the caterpillar into a butterfly as something gentle, almost poetic. And yet, the biological reality is far more violent. Inside the cocoon, the caterpillar does not transform progressively: it dissolves almost entirely. Its old structure disappears. What it was until then literally ceases to exist in its initial form.

And it is only at the heart of that invisible destruction, that total loss of bearings and identity, that another form slowly ends up emerging.

That is exactly what I lived through.

After the collapse, what had broken was not only financial. It was an entire way of inhabiting the world.

My certainties.

My definition of security.

My relationship with money.

And even the image I had of myself.

The real reconstruction was nothing spectacular. It did not begin in a great moment of strength or visible rebirth. It began in tiny gestures, almost invisible to others.

Opening each letter without letting the anguish paralyze me.

Looking at my accounts and my figures without averting my eyes.

Asking questions all the way through.

Finally learning what I had let other people manage in my place for years.

That is how I began, slowly, to rebuild something far deeper than my financial situation: my ability to fully inhabit my own life.

And above all, to accept a difficult truth: no one would come to rebuild my security in my place.

* * *

The first decision: paying myself

The reconstruction began with a simple gesture. Almost trivial in appearance. But one that changed everything.

With each paycheck, I began transferring a fixed sum to a separate account — an account I had opened only in my name, and that I forbade myself to touch. Not a fortune. Not an impressive amount. A reasonable sum, deliberately chosen to be sustainable over time.

This gesture, however small in appearance, carried something radically new for me: I was paying myself first. Before the groceries. Before the children. Before the unforeseen expenses. Before everything else.

For years, I had operated the other way around — I gave to everyone, I covered everything there was to cover, and if something was left at the end of the month, I kept it. But there was rarely anything left. And even when there was, that sum was not thought of as construction. It was a leftover. A residue. Not an intention.

That account I did not touch became something else. An anchor. The concrete proof, each month, that something was accumulating for me. Not for the family. Not for others. For me.

This change of sequence — paying myself first, then covering the rest — is one of the most transformative gestures I have ever made. Not because it made me rich immediately. But because it changed the way I perceived myself. I was no longer someone who managed what passed through. I was someone who was building.

* * *

What regularity does that intensity cannot

An investment of 200 francs a month for 20 years, with an average annual return of 5%, produces about 82,000 francs. The same total amount — 48,000 francs — invested all at once at the start produces about 127,000 francs, but only if you have that sum. Most people do not. What is accessible to almost everyone, on the other hand, is regularity. It is regularity that does the work over time. Not the starting amount. Not the perfect moment. Constancy.

The second step: putting money to work

Once that personal cushion began to exist — once I had the certainty that it was there, stable, protected, in my name — I could move to the next step.

Investing.

Not in something spectacular. Not in cryptocurrencies, leveraged products, or promising opportunities of double-digit returns. I had lived through what those promises could produce. I had no intention of repeating them.

My objective was simple, almost modest in its phrasing: to make my money work just above inflation. To beat the silent erosion that eats away at every franc left inactive. Nothing more. Safe, diversified investments, designed for the long term.

And that is where a truth imposed itself on me with a clarity I had not anticipated: my money was finally working for me. Not for someone else. Not for a project I did not fully understand. Not in the service of a vision that was not mine.

For me.

These two words may seem simple. They were not. After years of financing the family's daily life, of supporting other people's projects, of being absent from my own financial construction — seeing my money grow slowly, quietly, in a direction I had chosen, represented something immense.

It was not greed. It was not selfishness. It was presence. At last.

***

Inflation — the silent theft no one sees

In Switzerland, average inflation over the past twenty years is around 1 to 2% a year. That may seem low. But 2% a year means that 10,000 francs left in a non-interest-bearing account is actually worth less than 8,200 francs twenty years later in purchasing power. Financial inaction has a cost. It is invisible, gradual, and certain.

Investing just above inflation is not a modest ambition — it is the minimum condition for money not to lose value over time.

Deconstructing the belief

For a long time, I had believed that investment belonged to another category of people. Investors, in my imagination, were people already rich, already legitimate, who had grown up in families where wealth was discussed around the table. I knew how to work. I knew how to give. I knew how to support. But building wealth seemed to belong to a universe outside my own.

This belief is one of the greatest financial lies passed on to women.

Because in reality, most solid fortunes do not begin with fortunes. They begin with habits. Morgan Housel writes in The Psychology of Money with remarkable clarity: true financial security is often built silently, thanks to time, regularity, and the ability to defer certain immediate gratifications.

The question was no longer: how much do I have today? The real question was: what relationship am I building with money? Because it is not income that transforms a trajectory. It is repeated behaviors.

***

What women taught me

In that period, something else profoundly contributed to my reconstruction: the women I began to meet.

For the first time in my life, I was entering spaces where women spoke about money without awkwardness, without shame, without that strange tension that often accompanies women's financial conversations. They spoke about investment as a normal subject. They knew their figures. Some had been through extremely difficult divorces. Others were rebuilding after economic violence. But they all had one thing in common: they were present in their financial decisions.

Most women are not ignorant. They have simply been socialized to make money circulate rather than to build with it. They know how to nourish, organize, maintain, support. But very few learn to transform a part of what they earn into assets capable of protecting them in the future. This difference seems subtle. In reality, it changes an entire existence.

* * *

The relapse

Eighteen months after the separation, I was beginning to breathe.

The most urgent debts were repaid. I had opened my own accounts. I was reading. I was asking questions. I believed myself — sincerely — healed.

Then someone spoke to me about an investment opportunity.

It was not presented as something dubious or clandestine. On the contrary. The project seemed structured, coherent, carried by people who mastered their subject. The explanations were fluid. The discourse reassuring. Everything seemed serious.

And that is precisely where something deeper replayed itself in me.

I asked questions, of course. I had learned to do that. But when certain answers remained imprecise, I did not really insist. A part of me wanted to move forward. Wanted to believe that this new period of my life could finally be different. Wanted also to prove something to myself: that I was now capable of investing, of rebuilding, of taking back my place in my own financial life.

Deep down, though, a small voice persisted.

Is this really clear?

Have you understood enough?

Why do you still feel this doubt?

I heard it. But instead of fully listening to it, I chose to interpret it otherwise. As an excessive fear born of the past. As a trace of the previous trauma. Something to be overcome so as not to remain a prisoner of distrust.

So I signed.

The sum represented months of effort. Months spent slowly rebuilding what had been destroyed. Every franc saved had demanded silent sacrifices: fewer expenses, less comfort, outings declined, projects postponed, a life deliberately reduced to the essential.

And within a few months, everything vanished again.

The company eventually collapsed. Not in a spectacular scandal. Not in a fraud worthy of the newspapers. Just one bankruptcy among so many others. A "normal" bankruptcy, in which small investors often discover too late their real place in the chain of priorities.

But what struck me most that day was not only the financial loss.

It was the inner mechanism that had made that loss possible.

I thought I had learned no longer to trust blindly. And yet, instead of truly learning to understand, analyze, and decide for myself, I had again looked for someone to whom I could delegate a part of that responsibility. In a different form. More discreet. More sophisticated, perhaps. But the deep mechanism remained strangely the same.

I had just reproduced, on a more modest scale but with a far greater awareness, exactly what I had promised myself I would never relive.

I had not truly tried to understand in depth. I had still hoped that someone else would master in my place what I had not had the courage or the patience to learn fully myself.

Deep down, I wanted to go faster. To shorten the path. To be reassured, guided, convinced by an external certainty rather than slowly build my own conviction.

The voice that had warned me was the same voice that had fallen silent during the marriage. The same as the one that had fallen silent after the birth. A voice I had not yet learned to listen to — only to recognize after the fact.

This relapse taught me something that the first fall, on its own, had not yet taught me.

A conditioning does not disappear simply because you become aware of it. Seeing it is not enough to undo it.

It weakens only when you begin to act differently, consciously, repetition after repetition, until a new way of thinking, deciding, and protecting yourself finally becomes more natural than the old one.

True reconstruction is not an event. It is a practice.

And that inner voice that had tried to warn me that day — I eventually understood that it was neither a weakness nor an irrational fear to be fought.

It was probably one of the most precious instruments I still possessed.

Today, I listen to it. Even when it comes to thwart my desires, slow my impulses, or call into question what I would like to believe.

Especially when it disturbs me.

It was also at that moment that I understood why solid structures are so essential. The greatest financial disasters are not always born of ignorance or a lack of intelligence. They often appear when there are no longer enough counterweights, no one left to question, verify, slow down, or confront the decisions being made.

When an individual becomes alone before his convictions, his risks, his certainties, and his own blind spots, the boundary between confidence and drift can become dangerously fragile.

That is why today I deeply believe in a simple rule: never entrust your financial future to a lone wolf.

* * *

Passing it on differently

Then there were my children.

Without my even realizing it at first, something new began to be born in our house: a different way of talking about money.

Not in fear.

Not in anguish.

Not as a shameful or conflict-ridden subject to be avoided until the day everything explodes.

Simply a natural presence of these questions in our daily life. Simple conversations, suited to their age, where money ceased to be a taboo and became again what it should always have been: a subject of life, of responsibility, and of understanding.

One evening, my son asked me whether the purchase we were considering was a real need or simply a want.

That question, though simple, deeply moved me.

Because in that instant, I understood that what was being passed on in our house went far beyond money itself. It was not only a way of spending or saving. It was a consciousness being born. An ability to reflect, to distinguish the essential from the superfluous, to no longer experience consumption as an automatic reflex but as a choice.

True reconstruction is much deeper than recovering what one has lost. It consists in interrupting the silent transmission of certain patterns. In transforming a pain into a consciousness. In ensuring that what destroyed me does not become the invisible inheritance of my children.

***

What this chapter teaches — rules and actions

Taking back the power does not begin with a great decision. It begins with an automatic transfer, an account opened in your name, a sum deposited each month without touching it. Regularity does what intensity cannot.

Rule 43. Paying yourself first is not selfishness. It is a strategy. Before any expense, before any support to others, a fixed share of each paycheck must go toward your own security. This change of sequence — paying myself first, then covering the rest — is one of the most transformative gestures a woman can make.

Rule 44. Investing just above inflation is a real victory. You do not need to aim for extraordinary returns to build something solid. Beating the silent erosion of purchasing power, regularly, patiently, is enough to transform a trajectory over the long term.

Rule 45. You do not need to be rich to invest. You become rich because you invest — regularly, modestly, over time. The question is not how much you have today. It is what relationship you build with money starting today.

Rule 46. Never entrust your financial future to a lone wolf. Anyone who manages money — including yourself — needs an outside eye, a structure, a counterweight. The absence of contradiction is always a risk.

Rule 47. Passing financial consciousness on to your children is one of the most protective acts you can accomplish. Not anxiety. Not obsession. Consciousness — the kind that money is a tool, and that they are responsible for it.

Action 1. This month, open a savings account only in your name. Decide on a fixed amount — even 50 francs — that will automatically go to this account on the day of each paycheck, before any other expense. Do not touch it. Watch it grow. It is your first act of financial presence.

Action 2. To begin investing above inflation in Switzerland, explore the following options depending on your time horizon: the third pillar (VIAC or Finpension) for the retirement horizon, and a diversified world ETF such as VWRL on Swissquote or Yuh for a medium-term investment. These vehicles are simple, regulated, and designed for investors who do not wish to spend their lives watching the markets. The goal is not to become an expert. It is to stop letting your money sleep.

Action 3. Before entrusting money to anyone, ask these three questions without exception: Who supervises this person or this structure? What are the real fees, not the ones announced? What happens if I want to recover my money in six months? If the answers are vague — the money stays with you.

No one will build your security for you.

PART VII

What I pass on

Chapter 13 — The manifesto

Three truths. Three rules. One letter.

All that precedes is a story. One single story. Mine. What follows is what that story taught me — and what I would like to pass on to you, in a few rules, before you close this book.

There are books that bring answers. And there are books that force you to finally ask the right questions.

If you have made it this far, then I do not want to end with more theory. Life contains enough of that already. I simply want to leave here what I would have wanted to understand much earlier. Not perfect principles. But three rules capable, over time, of profoundly changing a trajectory.

It is not the amount one earns that protects. It is the way one thinks, structures, anticipates, and acts in the face of money.

* * *

1. Educate yourself. Always.

For a long time, I believed that love, loyalty, and trust were enough to protect a woman. I was wrong. Trust is precious. But trust that lives in ignorance becomes fragile. And sometimes dangerous.

No woman should sign documents she does not understand. No woman should be unaware of where the household money goes, what is invested, what is at risk, what is owed, what truly belongs to the couple, and what exists only in promises or projections. Financial ignorance does not only erode a bank account. It slowly erodes the capacity to freely choose one's life.

So learn. Not to become obsessed with money, but to never again be absent from a decision that commits your future. You do not need to master everything. But you must understand enough so that no one can think and decide entirely in your place.

***

2. Participate in decisions.

A couple is not a financial delegation. It is probably one of the most important things I learned through this story.

It does not matter who earns more. It does not matter who seems more competent. When a decision commits wealth, savings, debts, or the stability of a family — that decision belongs to both. Always.

Danger does not necessarily begin with bad intentions. It often begins at the moment when one person progressively stops looking, thinking the other already manages everything well. This belief seems harmless. And yet, it can contain a silent disappearance — a way of slowly leaving one's own financial life while believing one is simply trusting.

Healthy trust never excludes lucidity. Asking questions does not destroy a couple. Understanding does not threaten love. Participating does not mean controlling. It simply means staying present in the reality you are building together.

***

3. Invest. Now.

The greatest financial lie that many women carry within them is this: believing that investment naturally belongs to others. To experts. To men. To those who grew up in families where money was discussed around the table.

These barriers are not real. They are cultural. Psychological. Transmitted silently.

What studies show about women and investment

A Fidelity Investments study covering 5.2 million investment accounts revealed that women obtain on average returns 0.4% per year higher than men. Over twenty years, this difference can represent tens of thousands of francs. The main reason: women trade less frequently, take fewer impulsive risks, and stay invested longer in their strategies. The problem is therefore not a female inability to invest. It is a deficit of exposure, of confidence, and of early financial education.

Many women unconsciously think that investing requires being an expert, or having a lot of money to start with. Both beliefs are false.

Most solid fortunes do not begin with fortunes. They begin with habits. Modest but repeated decisions over years. One hundred francs invested regularly for twenty years has more power than a great project endlessly postponed. What transforms a financial trajectory is not punctual intensity — it is continuity.

An income allows you to live today. Wealth protects the future. It creates options. It allows you to breathe when life becomes harder. It reduces certain invisible dependencies. And above all, it gives time — which is probably the most precious form of wealth.

From the moment a woman begins to build something that truly belongs to her — even modestly — she progressively stops living only in the management of the present. She begins to project herself. To anticipate. To think in terms of the future.

And this transformation goes well beyond money.

***

Letter to Women

My dear reader,

For a long time, I believed that safety came from others. From a solid couple. From a competent man. From a stable income. From a life that seemed to stand upright.

And then one day, I understood something far more uncomfortable: a woman can be surrounded, loved, outwardly protected — and still remain profoundly vulnerable.

Because true security is not born only of what one possesses. It is born of what one understands.

***

If I wrote this book, it was not to recount a fall. Many women go through separations, losses, betrayals, financial collapses. My story has nothing exceptional in its pain.

What is rarer, on the other hand, is daring to look honestly at what these events reveal.

For a long time I thought that my greatest mistake had been to trust.

Today, I know it was not that. Trust is not a weakness.

What becomes dangerous is to disappear completely inside that trust. To let someone think, decide, understand, and anticipate in our place for so long that we ourselves end up silently leaving our own life.

And yet, no woman should live this way.

* * *

We learned to take care of others very early. To support. To hold. To repair. To absorb daily emergencies without stopping. Many of us know how to make an entire family function with remarkable strength.

But we have rarely been taught to ask ourselves: and me, what am I actually building?

Not only for today. For tomorrow. For the years when life will become more fragile. For the periods when love alone will no longer be enough to protect an existence.

* * *

I deeply believe that the financial education of women goes far beyond money.

It is about dignity. About inner freedom. About the capacity to choose. About peace.

It is also about transmission.

Because a child who grows up beside a woman present in her decisions learns something else about the world. He understands that security is built. That love and lucidity can coexist. That taking one's place is not an act of war — but an act of responsibility toward oneself.

* * *

I do not know what this book will awaken in you.

Perhaps simply a question you had been pushing aside for a long time. Perhaps a conversation you did not dare to have. Perhaps the need to finally look certain figures in the face. Or perhaps only that quiet sensation that something must now change.

Great transformations rarely begin in noise. They often begin in a very calm, almost invisible moment, when a woman decides inwardly that she no longer wants to live at a distance from herself.

* * *

If you are looking for one thing to do tonight, as you set this book down, here is what I suggest.

Not a grand gesture. The smallest one you can make.

Open your last bank statement. Not to judge it. Not to correct it. Simply to look at it for five minutes.

Note a question — only one — that you do not have the answer to.

That is all.

You have just begun.

* * *

And if that moment has arrived for you, then this book will have already accomplished its mission.

Christelle

Appendices

The Rules

Full list

Here, gathered in one place, are all the rules stated throughout this book. Keep this page within reach. Return to it when you have a decision to make. Print it if needed. These are the sentences I would have wanted to know fifteen years earlier.

* * *

1. Love does not replace financial presence. Trust should never mean absence, silence, or ignorance.

2. Savings without protection can disappear overnight. In whose name is the account? Who has access to it? What happens if the relationship changes?

3. Invisible work has real economic value. In Switzerland, a stay-at-home mother replaces on average between 90,000 and 120,000 francs of services per year.

4. Income does not automatically create wealth. Earning and building are two distinct skills.

5. Emotional spending can empty an entire financial life. Helping others without first reserving a portion for yourself leads to vulnerability.

6. Helping with awareness is not helping less. It is helping better. Pay yourself first, then give.

7. The first investment is identity, not finance. The day a portion of your money builds for you, your relationship with yourself changes.

8. Participating in daily life does not mean building wealth. Maintaining the household and building your security are two different gestures.

9. Love does not replace legal structure. A lack of love and a lack of structure are corrected differently.

10. A woman must always be building something that belongs to her. Not from distrust — from presence.

11. Financing a property that does not legally belong to you is not a contribution to the household. It is a gift without legal counterpart.

12. Appearance is a financial trap as much as a social one. Every franc spent to maintain an image is a franc that does not build.

13. Shame prevents action at the moment when action is most necessary. What you cannot say, you cannot solve.

14. Chronic financial anxiety is a signal, not a weakness.

15. Social comparison impoverishes — emotionally and financially.

16. Stopping work to raise a child has a precise, calculable, and often underestimated cost. It appears at age 65.

17. Part-time work erodes retirement provision invisibly. Below 22,050 francs of annual salary, the mandatory second pillar no longer exists.

18. The default matrimonial regime in Switzerland does not automatically protect invisible contribution.

19. One marriage in two ends in divorce. A woman's financial protection cannot rest solely on the duration of the marriage.

20. Trusting never exempts one from understanding.

21. Urgent decisions deserve even more attention than others. Taking twenty-four hours before signing is never a bad decision.

22. What you stop looking at ends up escaping you.

23. Listening to your financial intuition is not distrust. It is responsibility.

24. Postpartum depression can last months and go unnoticed. If you recognize these signs in yourself or in a woman close to you, seek help without waiting.

25. Asking for help is not failing. It is acting.

26. A couple becomes a family at the birth of a child. This shift requires a conscious reorganization — not only logistical, but decisional.

27. Repeated financial opacity is always a warning signal. Vague answers are not the sign of an overwhelmed partner. They are signals.

28. Participating in the financial decisions of your household is not a lack of trust. It is a responsibility.

29. Technical competence protects neither from denial, nor from ego, nor from risky behaviors.

30. A single person should never carry alone all the financial reality of a couple.

31. Joint tax liability exists even without conscious signature. Ignorance does not protect you before the administration.

32. Trusting is not delegating. You can love someone and still ask to see the accounts.

33. Emotional disconnection from money is a warning signal.

34. Recognizing your part is not punishing yourself. It is recovering your power.

35. Technical knowledge is not enough without active presence. Knowing is not looking.

36. A woman's legitimacy does not stop at the door of her home.

37. Being the same person everywhere is a strength. Coherence between the woman at the office and the woman at home is a protection no one can take away.

38. You do not rebuild on a debt you have not looked at. Inventory first. Invest later.

39. The order of reconstruction is fixed: assessment → debt repayment → emergency savings → investment.

40. Financial education is not reserved for experts. What is lacking is not capacity — it is exposure.

41. Forgiveness is part of financial reconstruction.

42. Surrounding yourself is not weakness. It is strategy.

43. Paying yourself first is not selfishness. It is strategy.

44. Investing just above inflation is a real victory.

45. You do not need to be rich to invest. You become rich because you invest.

46. Never entrust your financial future to a lone wolf. The absence of contradiction is always a risk.

47. Passing financial consciousness on to your children is one of the most protective acts you can accomplish.

Resources

To go further

What you read in a book is never enough on its own. These resources are the ones I would have wanted to have earlier — books that shift something, podcasts that normalize conversations about money, and concrete platforms for taking action in Switzerland.

This is not an exhaustive list. It is a starting point.

***

Books

On the psychology and behaviors of money

The Psychology of Money — Morgan Housel (2020)

The reference book on how our emotions, fears, and beliefs influence our financial decisions. Accessible, without jargon, deeply human. This is the first book I recommend to anyone beginning to take an interest in their financial life.

Rich Dad Poor Dad — Robert T. Kiyosaki

A global classic. It explains, through two opposing family models, why some people build wealth and others do not — independent of their income level. The distinction between assets and liabilities is explained in an unforgettable way.

The Millionaire Next Door — Thomas J. Stanley and William D. Danko

A study of American millionaires that reveals a counterintuitive truth: most truly wealthy people do not show it. They live simply, invest regularly, and build over time. An antidote to the culture of appearance.

All Your Worth — Elizabeth Warren and Amelia Warren Tyagi

The book at the origin of the 50/30/20 rule. Elizabeth Warren, former Harvard law professor and U.S. senator, explains how to structure your budget simply and sustainably. Practical, kind, written for ordinary people.

On money and women

Libérées — Titiou Lecoq (2017)

The essay that popularized the yogurt pots theory. Titiou Lecoq analyzes with humor and rigor the invisible inequalities that persist in modern couples — including financial inequalities. Indispensable reading for any woman who wants to understand the structural imbalances of her daily life.

Worth It: Your Life, Your Money, Your Terms — Amanda Steinberg

Founder of DailyWorth, Amanda Steinberg speaks directly to women who have always believed that money was not their domain. She dismantles this belief page after page with concrete tools and a deeply personal voice.

Clever Girl Finance — Bola Sokunbi

Written by a Black American woman for all women who have never had financial models that looked like them. Practical, encouraging, grounded in concrete realities. One of the rare personal finance books that also addresses the cultural and family dynamics around money.

On investment and wealth building

The Intelligent Investor — Benjamin Graham (with preface by Warren Buffett)

Considered the bible of value investing. More technical than the other books on this list, but fundamental for understanding the difference between speculating and investing. The chapter on "Mr. Market" remains one of the most powerful metaphors ever written on the psychology of markets.

Je veux de l'argent — Laure Prenat

A practical guide in French, written by a woman, for learning the basics of investment without drowning in jargon. Ideal for beginners who want to understand ETFs, real estate, and retirement without going through a bank advisor.

Atomic Habits — James Clear

Not a finance book — but perhaps the most useful on this list for building a solid financial life. James Clear demonstrates that it is not great decisions that transform a trajectory, but small repeated habits. Saving 100 francs per month for twenty years is an atomic habit. This book explains why it works.

* * *

Podcasts

In French

Émotions — Louie Media

Not a finance podcast, but one of the best French podcasts on psychology. Several episodes address our relationship with money, with safety, and with dependence — subjects directly linked to everything this book explores.

Entrepôt — Mathieu Stern

A French podcast on entrepreneurship and financial independence, accessible and concrete. Mathieu Stern interviews people who built their financial freedom from ordinary situations.

Café de Bourse — Café de la Bourse

A practical podcast on stock market investing, accessible to French-speaking beginners. Episodes cover the basics of ETFs, diversification, and portfolio management without unnecessary jargon.

In English

So Money — Farnoosh Torabi

One of the most respected voices in financial education for women. Farnoosh Torabi interviews finance personalities, entrepreneurs, and ordinary people about their relationship with money. Direct, kind, without taboo.

We Study Billionaires — The Investor's Podcast Network

For those who want to go further in understanding markets and investment strategies. Each episode analyzes the decisions of major investors — Warren Buffett, Charlie Munger, Ray Dalio — with remarkable pedagogy.

Afford Anything — Paula Pant

A podcast built around a simple idea: you can afford anything, but not everything at once. Paula Pant helps her listeners make conscious choices rather than being subject to their finances. Excellent introduction to real estate investing and financial freedom.

***

Investment platforms in Switzerland

These platforms are mentioned in the Actions throughout this book. They allow you to open an investment account from Switzerland, often in less than thirty minutes, with accessible starting amounts. They do not constitute personalized financial advice — every situation is different. For advice adapted to your reality, consult an independent financial advisor.

To begin investing

Swissquote — Switzerland · swissquote.ch

The leading online brokerage platform in Switzerland. Regulated by FINMA, it allows you to buy stocks, ETFs, bonds, and other financial products. Complete interface, suited to beginners as well as experienced investors. Brokerage fees starting at 9 CHF per transaction.

Yuh — Switzerland · yuh.com

Developed by PostFinance and Swissquote, Yuh is a mobile application designed for beginners. Intuitive interface, low fees, the possibility of investing from a few francs in ETFs and fractional shares. Ideal for a concrete and accessible first step.

Saxo Bank — Denmark / Switzerland · home.saxo/en-ch

An international platform available in Switzerland, offering a wide range of financial products including global ETFs. Professional interface with a well-designed beginner version. Competitive fees and access to diversified international markets.

For retirement and the third pillar

VIAC — Switzerland · viac.ch

The leading solution for the tied third pillar invested in the stock market (pillar 3a). VIAC offers portfolios composed primarily of low-cost ETFs, with fees among the lowest on the Swiss market. Recommended by many independent financial experts in Switzerland.

Finpension — Switzerland · finpension.ch

Direct competitor to VIAC for the third pillar, with advanced customization options and very competitive fees. Also available for free pension provision (pillar 3b). Ideal for people who want to maximize tax optimization while investing.

frankly — Switzerland · frankly.app

Mobile application developed by Zürcher Kantonalbank (ZKB) for the third pillar. Simple interface, integration with the Swiss banking system, good diversification in ETFs. A solid option for beginners who want to start investing their retirement savings.

To understand your financial situation in Switzerland

Moneyland — Switzerland · moneyland.ch

The leading independent comparison service in Switzerland. It allows you to compare bank accounts, insurance policies, mortgages, retirement solutions, and investment platforms. Free, without sponsored advertising, independently managed. An indispensable tool before any major financial decision.

Cantonal tax service — Switzerland · depending on your canton

An essential reminder: every Swiss canton has a tax service accessible by phone or online. In case of doubt about your tax situation, your joint declaration, your rights in case of separation, or your joint liability — contact your cantonal service directly. They are obligated to answer your questions. It is free.

***

Getting support

No book, no podcast, no platform replaces personalized support. If you are going through a separation, a financial reconstruction, or simply want to build a strategy adapted to your reality — seek an independent professional.

A few markers for choosing a good financial advisor in Switzerland

Independent advisor versus bank advisor

A bank advisor is paid by their bank — they may have an interest in recommending their institution's products. An independent financial advisor (or fee-only advisor) is paid only by you. Their recommendation is not influenced by commissions. In Switzerland, look for members of the Swiss Association of Asset Managers (ASG) or advisors certified as CFP (Certified Financial Planner).

Legal support in case of separation

For everything concerning the liquidation of the matrimonial regime, the division of the second pillar, joint debts, and tax rights after separation — consult a lawyer specialized in family law. The Bar Association of your canton publishes a directory accessible for free online.

Psychological support

A financial collapse is also an emotional collapse. If you are going through a difficult period, the Medico-Social Center (CMS) of your canton often offers free or low-cost consultations. Some Swiss health insurance providers also reimburse part of psychotherapy sessions.

* * *

These resources are a starting point, not a destination. What matters is to begin — even imperfectly, even with little. Because the only truly irreparable financial mistake is never to have started.

SheGrows Switzerland

What I built with what I had been through

This book tells how pain can become consciousness. SheGrows is what that consciousness produced.

After the collapse, after the three years of deconstruction, after learning to look my finances in the face — one realization imposed itself with a clarity I had not anticipated: what I had been through was not exceptional. Millions of women, all over the world, live within exactly the same financial invisibility. Not because they are incapable. Because no one has ever really given them the keys.

SheGrows was born of this conviction. Not to retell my story endlessly. But to transform that story into something useful — concrete, accessible, transmissible.

* * *

What SheGrows is

SheGrows Switzerland is a non-profit association, founded in Geneva in September 2025. Its mission is simple in its statement, demanding in its execution: to promote financial education, particularly among women, through training, workshops, mentoring, and concrete tools.

It is not a bank. It is not an investment advisory service. It is a space of education and empowerment — a place where women learn to understand their financial reality, to ask the right questions, and to make their own decisions with full awareness.

The name SheGrows is not a slogan. It is a conviction: a woman who understands her finances does not only grow financially. She grows in confidence, in freedom, in the capacity to choose her life.

***

The platform — Grow in Power

Alongside the association, SheGrows is developing a digital educational platform — the first designed to accompany women through the entirety of their financial life, not only through an isolated product or decision.

The platform is structured around the Seven Laws of Gold, drawn from The Richest Man in Babylon by George S. Clason — one of the most read and cited personal finance books in the world for nearly a century. These laws, four thousand years old, remain remarkably precise: save a portion of what you earn, control your expenses, make your money work, protect what you have built, prepare for retirement, invest in your capacity to earn more.

The platform translates these laws into concrete features, adapted to the Swiss reality and to the lives of women today.

***

The Seven Laws — alive in the platform

Law I — A part of what you earn belongs to you

Before any budget, before any spending, the platform sets aside 10% of your income. Your dashboard starts with what is yours — not with what you owe.

Law II — Control your expenses

You name your expenses yourself. The act of naming is where transformation begins. The platform reflects your habits — without ever lecturing you.

Law III — Make your money multiply

Every franc is visible as active money or dormant money. Dormant money has a visible monthly cost. Three options. One gesture to put it to work.

Law IV — Protect your wealth against loss

Before any investment, three questions. Does this product match your profile? Is it a proven vehicle? Do you actually understand it? Protection, not paternalism.

Law V — Make your home a profitable investment

Rent versus buy analysis, adapted to your city. Mortgage simulation. Value projection. Grounded in the market where you actually live.

Law VI — Ensure a future income

Your financial portrait at 45, 60, and 75. Three versions: if you change nothing, if you apply certain laws, if you apply them all. Your future, in real figures.

Law VII — Increase your capacity to earn

Most platforms treat your income as a constant. SheGrows treats it as your most important variable. Skills, salary benchmarks, negotiation preparation — adapted to your market.

* * *

A journey in five stages

The platform places each woman honestly — not where she would like to be, but where she actually is. Then it accompanies her.

The five stages of the SheGrows journey

Stage 1 — The Empty Purse: debts, no savings, financial fear. Protection activates first. The first tithe begins. The mirror reflects without judgment.

Stage 2 — The Apprentice: stable income, emerging savings. The first real investment options appear.

Stage 3 — The Builder: growing savings, first investments. Wealth begins to take shape.

Stage 4 — The Merchant: multiple sources of income, growing portfolio. The full command center opens.

Stage 5 — The Sovereign: financial freedom, building a legacy. Transmission begins. You teach. You guide. You become.

* * *

What this book and SheGrows share

This book and SheGrows were born in the same place. From the same conviction, crossed through the same pain.

The conviction that the financial education of women is not a question of numbers. It is a question of dignity. Of freedom. Of the capacity to choose. And of transmission — because every woman who finally understands her financial reality changes something for her children, for those close to her, for the women who observe her without daring to ask the question.

This book is the narrative version of what SheGrows wants to build. SheGrows is the active version of what this book teaches. The one and the other pursue the same goal: that no woman discover too late what she could have understood much earlier.

* * *

Joining SheGrows

SheGrows Switzerland is open to anyone — woman or man — who shares the conviction that financial education is a tool of emancipation, not a privilege reserved for a few.

The digital platform is under development and will launch in the fourth quarter of 2026. Founding members will receive 50% off the first year and will receive immediately the series of the Seven Letters from Babylon — seven weekly texts, one per law, to begin the journey before the official launch.

To join the waiting list, follow the association's activities in Geneva, or learn more about the mission of SheGrows:

shegrows.ch

About the author

Christelle Donhossou is a finance professional based in Geneva, specialized in investment risk management and investor protection within international private banking.

Holder of a Master's in financial audit as well as a Master's in accounting and finance, she began her career in financial and regulatory audit before moving toward functions linked to compliance, governance, and investment risk. For nearly twenty years, she has worked at the heart of the financial markets and engages with the issues surrounding investor protection, financial products, and wealth management mechanisms.

Born in Benin and having grown up across several countries following her father's diplomatic career, she developed an international outlook early on, nourished by different cultures, economic realities, and ways of thinking about money.

Alongside her career, she is committed to better financial education for women. In 2025, she founded SheGrows Switzerland, a Geneva-based initiative dedicated to making finance more accessible, more understandable, and more concrete for women who wish to fully reclaim their place in their own financial decisions.

Through her work, her workshops, and her public speaking, she defends a simple idea: financial education is not reserved for experts, but is an essential tool of autonomy, protection, and freedom.

Start Now is her first book.

About the author

www.ingramcontent.com/pod-product-compliance
Lightning Source LLC
LaVergne TN
LVHW040515210926
848480LV00005BA/1469